POWER
OF
AGEING

A Guide for the
Second Half of Life[1]

ADAM DUNCAN

Copyright © 2020 by Adam Duncan

All rights reserved. No part of this publication may be reproduced, stored or transmitted in any form or by any means, electronic, mechanical, photocopying, recording, scanning, or otherwise without written permission from the publisher. It is illegal to copy this book, post it to a website, or distribute it by any other means without permission.

Adam Duncan asserts the moral right to be identified as the author of this work.

Adam Duncan has no responsibility for the persistence or accuracy of URLs for external or third-party Internet Websites referred to in this publication and does not guarantee that any content on such Websites is, or will remain, accurate or appropriate.

ISBN 9798686799981

First edition

Published by GINKGO MEDIA LTD 2020

Page layout by Chapter One Book Production, Knebworth, UK

In grateful memory of

PEGGY CLARE DUNCAN

1927–2016

The compensation of growing old, Peter Walsh thought, coming out of Regent's Park, and holding his hat in hand, was simply this; that the passions remain as strong as ever, but one has gained – at last! – the power which adds the supreme flavour to existence – the power of taking hold of experience, of turning it round, slowly, in the light."

—Virginia Woolf, *Mrs. Dalloway*

CONTENTS

ACKNOWLEDGMENTS	1
FOREWORD	3
PREFACE	5
INTRODUCTION Ageing offers greater opportunity to access our inner power	9
EARLY STAGES Going from dependent child to an independent individual	19
INTERDEPENDENCE Evolving to a mature adult through a deep experience of inter-connection	35
ARRESTED DEVELOPMENT Fearing old age and death, prevents further development and leads to isolation	41
THE TRANSITION Moving on from a confined world view is challenging but necessary to access power	55
TRAVELLING LIGHT Preparing for the journey by acknowledging loss	63

THE GREAT MYSTERY Opening up to the mystery of life, enables great benefit	73
THE FEAR OF DEATH Overcoming the fight, flight or freeze response mechanism	81
THE SEED OF INTENTION Finding your deep purpose in the present and in the future	97
PLANTING THE SEED Taking care to plant the seed of intention so that it takes root	119
TENDING THE SHOOTS Supporting your intention, no matter what difficulties may occur	123
HARVESTING THE FLOWERS AND FRUITS Becoming a healthy and healing elder in the face of uncertainty	133
AFTERWORD	143
FURTHER READING	147
WEBSITES	155
APPENDIX	157
ENDNOTES	159

ACKNOWLEDGEMENTS

In March 2020, due to the Covid pandemic, we had to cancel our scheduled *The Power of Ageing* courses and workshops. After the success of our workshops the previous year, we had been looking forward to taking the programme out to a wider audience. It was devastating when 'lock-down' struck, but the period of isolation that followed was ideal for writing this book. There were fewer distractions and no slipping out for coffee when the going got tough!

Seven months on, and I missed the joy of working face-to-face with all the wonderful people who supported the work. There were some still in their 40s and others in their 70s who came together harmoniously to explore transforming concerns around ageing and death into connection and purpose. Their open-minded generosity encouraged me to keep developing *The Power of Ageing* programme in whatever format I could. So, I owe a debt of gratitude to all of those who participated in the workshops. I hope we get to be together again soon.

I also thank my co-facilitators; Cathy Warren, Spencer Thomas, David Pugsly and especially Felice Rhiannon who co-designed the original Ageing-into-Eldering workshops. Thanks to Sally Garrett for her support through all of the workshops and to Nicola Glinwood for her encouragement. I'm grateful to Jamie Martin, actor and director, who showed trust in an earlier incarnation of this work.

There are other pioneers who have helped me on my way, including Shivam O'Brien of the Spirit Horse Community, Michael Boyle, Rex Brangwyn and Hugh Newton from A Band of Brothers, and Hermione Elliott and Alizoun Dickinson from End of Life Doula, UK.

Finally, I offer respect and gratitude to the many Buddhist pioneers who have helped me and especially Daisaku Ikeda, on whose broad shoulders I stand.

FOREWORD

by Aaron Swartz

There was a time in my fifties, when I was looking in the mirror, stretching my face back and trying to see what I would look like if I had plastic surgery. Such was my attachment to looking younger, but part of me knew that trying to recapture my youth was a sure way to isolation and loneliness.

I'm 62 now, and I've seen the demise of the older generations. I understand the inevitability of my own ageing and death, and it makes me reflect on my present existence. This is a wonderful gift! It enables me to appreciate my life and take nothing for granted. Like every other human, I am subject to the second law of thermodynamics, and yet instead of it making me feel defenceless and weak, my vulnerability can connect me to others and to a sense of joy.

I know it's easy to slip into fear and doubt about the future. We might drift into using coping strategies that don't serve us, but I also know that if we have connections and conversations with others around ageing and death, something remarkable happens! A most soulful and supportive experience can take place.

There may be no answers to our questions, but when one opens up to this 'final frontier', an expansive and beautiful experience is possible. This conversation can release us from all the petty worries and attachments we find taking up so much of our time. My conversations with others around death have done exactly that.

Attending Adam Duncan's workshops, and now reading his book, have allowed this most beautiful, intimate, and remarkable experience to happen. Rather being a morbid affair, each time we came together, there was a lightness in the air, sometimes laughter, at other times tears. We may be alone in death, but sharing the 'unspeakable', brought us paradoxically closer and perhaps most importantly, closer to ourselves and to the beauty of life.

Adam Duncan has been sharing his insights and his longing to open up this conversation with as many people as possible. It might be the most important conversation of our lives!

Aaron Swartz
MBACP, UKCP reg,
Somatic Experiencer Practioner, CRM

PREFACE

Hearing the call

It was a dull day in September 2016 when I started this new stage in my life. My mother lay asleep in the hospice. She was dying slowly. Fighting as she always had done, and not wanting to let go. To me, at that time, the hospice felt like a sacred, otherworldly place. There was an acceptance of death that I found intriguing. Here I was in the land of the dying, where the medics and volunteers went about their work with a calm good humour. Although I felt emotional about the end of my mother's life, I also felt reassured that she had good people caring for her.

I waited all morning in a kind of tranquil limbo hoping to connect with my dying mother. At lunchtime I went to the shopping centre to get something to eat in the canteen of a department store. After I had chosen a sandwich and a cup of tea, I noticed the cashier. It was as though all the life had been drained out of her. She was on autopilot. She was probably in her forties but to me, in my heightened emotional state, the cashier looked as though she had died a long time ago. While I ate my sandwich, I looked around the canteen and what I saw was quite shocking. It seemed as though the place was full of the undead. It felt as though there was no humanity here at all. There were just functional efficiencies and bleak transactions. From where I was sitting, the staff and the customers in the canteen all looked like extras in a zombie film. There was neither life nor death in the shopping centre. Just the undead. I wanted to get back to the love and compassion in the hospice - where life and death were acknowledged. Where people were valued no matter what state they were in.

For many years I had given occasional talks on Buddhist philosophy and I had studied texts about death and dying, but now I had an urgency to go deeper. It was this experience around my mother's death that made me do a foundation course with an organisation that trained 'death doulas[2]'. These are people who give non-clinical support to those who are dying and their families. The other participants on the course were all ages and from all walks of life, and some of them were hospice workers. I felt I had met a truly interesting tribe of people who understood and valued the transience of life. I experienced a burst of creative energy and confidence that I had not experienced since my youth. I wrote a theatre piece called *Seven Ages and the Dance of Life and Death*, and with actors, musicians and dancers, we put on fourteen performances. It was a joyous experience for us all, but I had a longing to go deeper into how we could live vibrantly and harmoniously in the second half of life by accepting the transience of life.

INTRODUCTION

Ageing offers greater opportunity to access our inner power

We are the survivors. We've experienced a good deal of life and have known some ups and down. We've been through the storms of youth and of middle age. And now, we find ourselves in an undefined stage of being. We may still be in our late 40s and dealing with the cut and thrust of life or we may be retired in our late 60s or 70s. We've taken at least 400 million breaths[3] so far and we're planning on taking a lot more. We have gained some wisdom over the years, yet remain creative and 'young at heart'. We have known some losses. Our youth has long gone, and middle age is starting to slip over the horizon, and yet in our minds we are not old. We have ideas and thoughts that would have been beyond the scope of our immature brain. Perhaps the ambitions and dreams of our youth no longer motivate us as they once did, but we suspect we still have something wonderful to offer. We see younger generations coming up behind us who think that anyone over 40 is ancient. They believe that sex, fashion and music are the exclusive preserve of their generation (just as we did at their age). As we grow older, we become more aware of the effects of ageing on the generations in front of us. The lively uncles and aunts of our childhood have become elderly. The grandparents start to disappear. In the second half of life, the ticking of the clock begins to get louder. Time seems to move faster now than in our youth. So much has already happened, and our lives are more than partially formed, and yet so much lies ahead of us.

So, congratulations on making this far! But the key question is, how do we make the most of each day in this phase of our life? Surely it has to be more than just survival! How do we deal with our concerns around ageing, and what preparations can we make for a sparkling and dynamic end of life? How do we deal emotionally with this part of the journey? How do we let go of the past and find meaning in the present? How can we find enthusiasm for the future?

Some 200 years ago the average age of death was around 40[4]. We have an increased life span today and can expect to live longer than previous generations, but despite the hopes of some scientists, our life is finite. We are fortunate to have more longevity, but what do we do with this extra time? We might want to live longer, but we don't want to get any older! For most of us, ageing brings up some concerns. We may have anxieties about our physical or mental capabilities diminishing, or about becoming useless to family, friends and society. We may dread being cut off and lonely. But do we have to be helpless victims in the face of ageing and mortality? So, what can we do?

Inner Power

Many of us find distractions and coping mechanisms to prevent us dwelling on our ageing process for too long. It is easy to slip into a closed mindset and habitual behaviour. The message of this book is that in the second half of life we have a wonderful opportunity to develop our inner power which can bring about healing and joy. To really make the most of our journey, we require our inner power which consists of three qualities that we all possess. Innate wisdom, compassion and courage are in every one of us no matter what our race or gender. It doesn't matter what we have done with our life up until this moment, we have these qualities. Whether we have lived a life of reckless debauchery or saintly discipline, we all carry this inner power within us. It's not in a sacred building or in a shaman or a guru. We won't find it on the mountain top or in a retreat centre. It is in each of us, no matter what our religious beliefs. The atheist, the agnostic and the worshipper all have it. It is a natural resource we human beings are fortunate to possess. And it is awesome! Mind-bogglingly awesome! It may lie buried deep within us or it may be close to the surface. It may be operational on a regular basis or your true inner power may never have seen active service. This book is how we can access this power now and right up to our dying breath.

It is not the amount of time we have left on this earth, but what we do with it, that gives us power. To agonise over what steps we should take as we grow older and worry excessively about our demise makes us impotent. Everyone has vast resources of courage and wisdom inside, but these qualities cannot be accessed with the handbrake on. It is only when we take action and stop living in fear that our highest qualities can be manifest.

We need the three qualities of innate wisdom, compassion and courage to work together for us to be fully in our power. Wisdom and compassion without courage, for example, may lack depth and effectiveness but with all three qualities working together as our inner power, we can feel happiness and well-being regardless of the situation or circumstances. There are bound to be problems as we age, but each challenge can enable us to deepen our confidence in our own power, so that we fully enjoy our journey as we get older.

Our inner power is not always easy to access. Many people are unaware that they carry such power inside. If they were to realise this force, I believe there would be less human suffering and environmental destruction in the world. This jewel is hidden in the very depths of our being. Invisible and amorphous. In myths and stories, the location of the treasure is traditionally guarded by monsters and demons. The heroine or hero has to go on an arduous and dangerous journey to gain their reward. Their dedication and commitment are tested again and again.

The Quest

In the second half of life we have the option to embark on a quest for our inner power. It's an adventure that involves both slowing down and speeding up. It involves being both in the present moment and in the future. This book aims to be a practical manual that supports us on our quest. It's an exciting drama that is open to people of all faiths, or no faith at all. It requires nothing but an open and questioning mind, along with some self-reflection and commitment.

This journey is not so suited to younger people – they have their own path to take. But by completing our own rite of passage we will be supporting younger generations in the most natural and powerful way.

In the following pages I share the formula for maximising our inner power which involves four crucial elements:

- an interdependent perspective on life
- our present breath
- our final breath
- our life intention

So, can we re-think later life? Can it be an opportunity to connect with our deeper nature and with each other? What will we leave behind us for the next generation? Despair, a broken society and ruined planet? Or can we start a social revolution? We have experience, and perhaps a little wisdom. With some work we can surely empower ourselves and start to transform the paradigm of ageing and death.

Exercises

The book aims to take you on a journey stage by stage, so that by chapter 10, you are ready to plant an intention in your life. You are encouraged to deepen your experience by keeping a journal and completing the exercises that are in some of the chapters. If you believe that you already have a clear life purpose that is serving you, then I hope the book will help strengthen your intention.

Case Studies

There are some short experiences and stories in some of the chapters. The names have been changed but they are all based on actual events.

Workshops and Courses

There are on-line and venue-based courses that explore some of the material in this book at www.powerofageing.com.

GRACE'S STORY: The need for transformation

In her twenties Grace moved to London and was asked by her mother to visit an ageing relative who lived in a wealthy suburb of the city. She'd never met her great aunt before, but bought some fruit and chocolate as an offering.

When she entered the big house, it was almost dark and Grace could hardly see her aged relative, so she went to turn the light on. Immediately the aunt snapped at her to turn it off. I haven't got money to burn on electricity, were the old woman's exact words. Grace listened to her great aunt's complaints for a while, but didn't stay long. Two years later the woman died leaving her two million pound inheritance to a cat's home.

By the time she was fifty-five her parents, uncles and aunts had all died in what Grace thought to be torment and anguish. She wondered if this kind of miserable old age and death was inevitable for her as well.

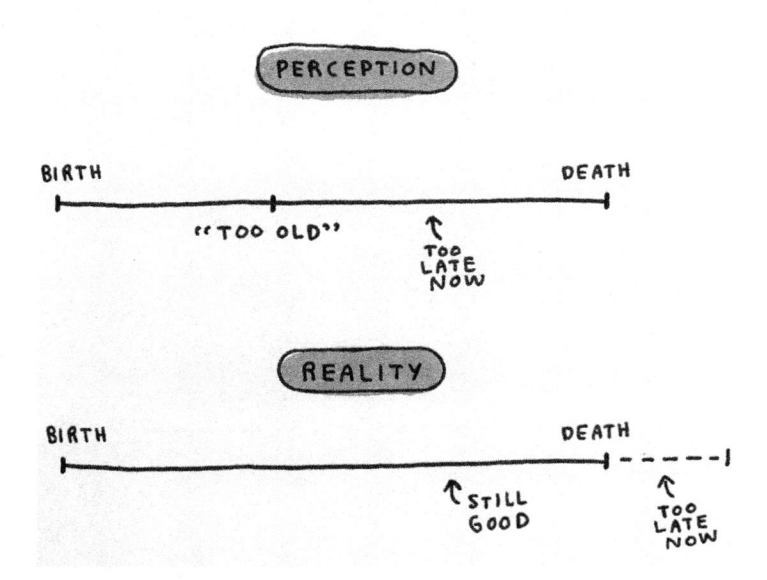

'Is it too late to start?'
Illustration by Michelle Rial

EARLY STAGES

Going from dependent child to an independent individual

It is quite normal to have concerns about ageing and it is a natural instinct for us to fear death. But the way we live in our society encourages and endorses a particular way of viewing life that amplifies and distorts our fear. Growing older in a culture that priorities separation and independence is a difficult and sad experience for some. However, we have the opportunity to go beyond the limitations of the independent mindset to fully access our inner power. But first, let's look at how we managed to make it this far in life.

Dependent Child

We started the ageing process as a single cell which forms when a sperm fertilises our mother's egg. And around three weeks later we have a beating heart. What was it like for us as our brain started to become active after five or six weeks? Does any part of us retain a sense of those early days as our physical and mental development rapidly progressed until we found that we had no room to move in the uterus? For those first nine months we were totally dependent on our mother, and then we were expelled from our 98.6° environment down the birth canal into the next stage of life.

If we are fortunate, there are three key stages in the development of our world view; dependent, independent and interdependent. Up to our teenage years, we were mostly dependent on others for our basic physical and emotional needs. If we were lucky, we grew into a child that was inquisitive, curious and able to open up to the wonder and mystery of life. We saw things mostly in the short term and it took forever for birthdays to come around. Time was in slow motion. We had a small radius of perception of the world, with little awareness of the complex connections that ran through life. By 12, the ageing process was well under way. We had already passed the first of many cognitive peaks – for example, the optimum time[5] to learn a new language is under the age of 10.

We may have known the loss of a pet or a relative for the first time. We became more aware of the outside world and how we fitted into it. Our radius of perception widened as time started to go just a little bit quicker. We were growing up and we knew big changes were afoot. In the wide world the position of women, gays and lesbians was being challenged. There was a revolution in music and fashion. Despite the development of the Cold War and nuclear weapons, many of us were optimistic about the chance of having a better world in the future. There was an expectation that technology and democracy would create a golden age by the 21st century.

By our mid-teens, the education system encouraged us to decide whether we were going to pursue the arts, the sciences or a trade. And for a generation of girls who grew up in the 1960s and 1970s there was also home economics! The question our culture was asking us was; 'How were we going to fit into the adult world?'

At the age of 18 we were statistically at the height of our brain processing powers which was just as well because we were about to enter an adult world which was complex and vast beyond our youthful imagination.

Independent Adult

It may not have been a picnic for our ancestors, but life was relatively simple back before the industrial and technological revolutions. In indigenous societies, the young adult had a sense of the boundaries of his world and what they contained. Growing up in the second half of the 20th century we stepped into a tangled confusion of challenges and feelings with some optimism but little preparation. Too many of our elders were killed or scarred by the horrors of two world wars and the ending of the British Empire. Any certainties from their colonial past were evaporating and people didn't understand the world that was emerging in the 1960s and 1970s. What help could our older role models give us? What words of wisdom as we said goodbye to childhood? There was no formal initiation that would support us as we set out on our journey to become a fully functioning adult.

As we progressed into the adult world, our initial career choices were made. Some of us specialised and focused on one particular area, such as teaching or servicing central-heating systems. It made sense to define our field of learning and detach it from the complex web of information that surrounded it. It created boundaries for us, and we developed an expertise and competence, so that we could have a quantifiable value in society. And with this came a burgeoning social identity, be it teacher, electrician, housewife or unemployed artist. If we could prove our credibility, we could also get a mortgage and get on the property ladder. At this stage in life it made a lot of sense to separate out our identity and skill-base.

The specialist education system allows society to function efficiently and to develop new and complex organisations. Without specialization, there would be no supermarkets and no national health service. There would be no sophisticated transport system, and many aspects of our world would cease to function. Separation, limits and boundaries can serve us. However, as we grow older, do we still want to be using the ingrained mindset that might have served us well when we were younger? As we will see there are some fundamental limitations to dividing life up and compartmentalising it.

This segmented view of life is supported by traditional science. The Newtonian or mechanistic view of life is sometimes known as reductionism[6] which states that if you want to know how something works, you reduce the system or organism to its most basic form. Then, if you study how each building block of the system behaves independently, you can determine how the whole system works. This sounds logical, and reductionism has produced some extraordinary discoveries such as the atomic structure of matter and the revolution in molecular biology. Many of the developments in psychology, economics and sociology come from studying a phenomenon that is isolated from its context or environment. But increasingly scientists are realising that you cannot always predict the behaviour of something by isolating it. Quarks[7], for example, combine to form composite particles called hadrons, but it has proved impossible for scientists to view a quark in isolation and in quantum mechanics[8] the mere act of observing an object affects the findings. Reductionism may be useful up to a point, but viewing ourselves or anything else in life as separate from the environment is ultimately a limited way of looking at the world. Viewing life only through the lens independence can cause great suffering, particularly as we get older.

There are limitations to separating out elements of a very complex system in order to predict results. For example, no one knows what the weather will be like in three weeks from now. There are simply too many variables. It is hard to conceive that a butterfly flapping its wings on the other side of the world could affect our weather[9]. There will be always be limitations to studying any complex system such as the human mind if we see it as separate from its environment.

In the first half of life we learnt to survive in a world that has many different compartments that are not always connected. Home. Work. Family. Finances. Friends. Each of these areas in our life is divided up into further separate categories. We had to separate to survive. Most of us were keenly aware that the emotional and physical dependence that was acceptable as a child was not appropriate in this adult world. Vulnerability was seen as a weakness. The struggle to become an independent adult may have involved hiding some parts of ourselves that no longer seemed appropriate. We had to 'fit in' rather than 'fit together'.

We may have adopted labels and identities in order to function efficiently in the competitive world, and so that other people could categorise us easily. To be self-contained and not to need support was seen as a good thing. We had to stand on our own two feet and fend for ourselves especially if we were a male. We had the role model of the lone wolf. The manipulative and controlling behaviour of politicians and the captains of industry appeared to be acceptable, and even admired by the media. We watched as the hero of the big screen who battled on his own against all the odds, won the day. You, too, had to become independent and be your own man.

As the women's movement emerged in the 1960s, there were calls for liberation and independence from the patriarchy. According to research, women were at their most physically attractive in their early 20s. They were desired or envied by older people and the new ideal was to be a strong, independent woman. Developing a state of independence was a survival mechanism but it was also an illusion to help us build, protect and nurture our youthful hopes and dreams.

Entering middle age

By our mid-30s, our physical prime was behind us and by our 40s, the volume of our brain[10] and its weight started to decline at a rate of around 5% per decade (although this doesn't necessarily equate to a corresponding decline in actual performance!).

It's around mid-life, though, that many start to realise just how youth-orientated their society is. But most people were too busy in the cut and thrust of life to worry too much about getting older. And life wasn't all bad. Our earning capacity was increasing. In fact, some people perceived us as being at the pinnacle of the human journey in our 30s and 40s, for it is around this time that workers tend to be most valued[11] and respected by institutions and employers. They have lost the impetuousness of youth, but they still had potential and a shelf-life. They had experience on which to make sensible decisions. They had responsibilities and plenty to lose, so they are often seen as good, reliable worker material.

But as the 40s progressed into the 50s and beyond, in a mad dash through middle age, we slowly woke up to the fact that we really were getting older. Those people with money and a secure job were encouraged to check out their pension and make sure that they had got a good investment portfolio and health insurance for their retirement.

And the rest of us? How would we survive in the late afternoon of life? We might look forward to taking our place in the pantheon of wise elders. We might spend our time fostering younger minds, but unfortunately wisdom doesn't necessarily come with age. And even if we had wisdom, the younger generations don't want to listen us. They've got enough on their plate. They've got their own priorities and we would do well to check our own. What is it that we need now that we're older? Are the needs the same as in our youth?

Our Needs

We can practice living in the present moment, but staying in 'the now' is hard even in the most idyllic surroundings. We can calm the mind but survival and functioning in our complex world involves some planning for the future. Even if we live in secluded cloisters, we all have desires and needs that take us out of the present moment. At the most basic level we desire to do more living and that entails the need for food, water, warmth, rest, security and safety. These are the bottom two lines on Maslow's hierarchy of needs, a five-tier pyramid of human needs from basic to developed, proposed by American psychologist Abraham Maslow[12] in 1943.

```
                    self-
               actualization
           morality, creativity,
          spontaneity, acceptance,
            experience purpose,
         meaning and inner potential
              self-esteem
    confidence, achievement, respect of others,
         the need to be a unique individual
            love and belonging
     friendship, family, intimacy, sense of connection
           safety and security
   health, employment, property, family and social stability
             physiological needs
     breathing, food, water, shelter, clothing, sleep
```

The need for life and the fear of death are hard-wired into us. The function of the reptilian part of our brain is to keep us alive. It controls our body's vital functions such as reflexive behaviours, heart rate, breathing and body temperature. It is a primal instinct to fear death and it is safe to say that around 99.9% of the world's population want to avoid the act of dying, a fear known as thanatophobia. While around 0.01 per cent of people commit suicide[13] in the UK each year, we are heavily programmed to avoid death. We will go to extraordinary lengths to avoid dying. No matter what we have to endure, we want to escape death at all costs. In the face of mortality, the independently-minded individual often develops one of the following responses to the threat of death;

- **The fight response** – a nihilistic hedonism that involves getting the most out of life while they can. Any meaningful discussion about ageing and the end of life is generally taboo.
- **The flight response** – stops us living a full life in the present due to a faith in an after-life or in a scientific breakthrough to ensure immortality.
- **The freeze response** – a numbing of natural energy and emotions that increases with age.

Such responses are triggered by the reptilian brain and the ego that have no understanding that life and death are two sides of the same coin. There can be no life without death. Without the death of bacteria, microbes, plants and trees, insects, birds, fish, mammals and especially humans, the planet would be overrun with life. Within a few weeks all life on earth would cease to function. We live in an ecosystem that necessitates death, but the independently-minded individual sees themselves as separate from the natural laws of life. Some billionaires don't want to be separated from their wealth and invest in scientific and pharmaceutical companies so they can develop solutions for longevity and immortality. It's a booming business but re-coding DNA is more likely to lead to eternal isolation and misery than to happiness.

The flight or fight response is a natural reaction to having our needs threatened. But is there any way we can better adapt to this perceived threat?

EXERCISE 1 Prioritising Our Needs

As we grow older, we might want to adjust Maslow's Hierarchy of Needs to reflect our priorities at this stage of our journey. Using the table below, prioritise in your journal what is important to you at this stage in your life. What are your needs?

Physiological Needs
These are biological requirements for human survival, e.g. air, food, drink, shelter, clothing, warmth, sex, sleep. If these needs are not satisfied the human body cannot function optimally. Maslow considered physiological needs the most important as all the other needs become secondary until these needs are met.

Safety Needs
Once an individual's physiological needs are satisfied, the needs for security and safety become salient. People want to experience order, predictability and control in their lives. These needs can be fulfilled by the family and society (e.g. police,

schools, business and medical care) For example, emotional security, financial security (e.g. employment, social welfare), law and order, freedom from fear, social stability, property, health and wellbeing (e.g. safety against accidents and injury).

Love and belongingness needs
The third level of human needs is social and involves feelings of belongingness. The need for interpersonal relationships motivates behaviour. Examples include friendship, intimacy, trust, and acceptance, receiving and giving affection and love. Affiliating, being part of a group (family, friends, work).

Esteem Needs
Maslow classifies two categories: (i) esteem for oneself (dignity, achievement, mastery, independence) and (ii) the desire for reputation or respect from others (e.g., status, prestige). Maslow indicated that the need for respect or reputation is most important for children and adolescents and precedes real self-esteem or dignity.

Self-actualization Needs
The highest level in Maslow's hierarchy, and refer to the realization of a person's potential,

> self-fulfillment, seeking personal growth and peak experiences. Maslow describes this level as the desire to accomplish everything that one can, to become the most that one can be. Individuals may perceive or focus on this need very specifically. For example, one individual may have a strong desire to become an ideal parent. In another, the desire may be expressed economically, academically or athletically. For others, it may be expressed creatively, in paintings, pictures, or inventions.

Fortunately, the stage of separation and independence is not the end of our journey. While it appears that there a basic human need for separation, there is also a need and a longing for connection. In *The Selfish Gene*, first published in 1976, the biologist Richard Dawkins claimed that we are genetically programmed to be selfish and it is this that has enabled human development. The book caused controversy and debate. One of Dawkins' tutors[14] at Oxford University called it a 'young man's book' implying that Dawkins had only presented a partial truth. In the first half of life we had a strong incentive to separate out elements of our life so that we could identify and control what we needed to. But there is also a strong emotional human need to connect up. To put things together. To join the dots.

To meet for coffee. To take the dog for a walk. To talk to a neighbour. And to see the bigger picture.

> ### RALPH'S STORY: A glimpse of the future
>
> For twenty years Ralph had taught English Literature at a sixth form college where his positive attitude and charisma were admired by most of his young students. It was the first week of the summer holidays after a hectic end of term when Ralph got a call from his sister. She told him that their mother was struggling with independent living and they had to start looking at what options there were for her future.
>
> Ralph felt mildly irritated when a couple of days later he set off in the car to check out one of the care homes. On the journey he kept asking himself what was his responsibility for his mother who had the earlier stages of Alzheimer's. While he was trying to come to terms with how he would cope with his ageing mother, he missed the turning to the care home twice.
>
> Ralph's sister had given him a list of questions to ask the manager about the facilities before Ralph was given a tour of the communal areas. Having spent much of his working life with lively 17 year olds, Ralph found it disturbing to see all the elderly and frail people eating lunch together.

> On the return journey, Ralph wondered about the staff redundancies at the college and his own future. By the time he arrived back home, he felt his life might be about to spiral out of control.

INTERDEPENDENCE

Evolving to a mature adult through a deep experience of interconnection

Independence and separation are only one side of the story. Since the publication of The Selfish Gene there have been many studies showing the basic need for human connection. In the 1990s two scientists in Italy, Giacomo Rizzolatti and Vittorio Gallese discovered 'mirror neurons'[15] which indicated that we have a natural ability to recognize the feelings and intentions of others. In other words, we are fundamentally empathic. These mirror neurons were called 'the basis of civilisation' by V.S. Ramachandran, professor of neuroscience at the University of California.

If we've spent the first half of our life in a culture that encourages separation, control and independence, the chances are we will be left with a fragmented or partial view of the life. But we have the opportunity to move on and to bring aspects of our lives together again.

It is important to start connecting up some of the fragmented pieces of our mind, body and soul because if we go into old age with a divided self, it can be painfully difficult. The mindset that served us as a young adult will not necessarily help us find joy and power as we age. A reductionist view of the world may have been functional at the time, but it is severely limited as we grow older and often leads to loneliness and isolation. But most importantly, if we stay in the independent and specialised stage of development, we risk missing the benefits of growing older. In the second half of life the process of reconnection can transform our fear of death and our anxiety about living. Putting together the pieces to form a holistic view of life can be a thrilling experience!

The opposite of reductionism in science is the theory of holism. The Oxford Dictionary defines this as 'The theory that parts of a whole are in intimate interconnection, such that they cannot exist independently of the whole, or cannot be understood without reference to the whole, which is thus regarded as greater than the sum of its parts.'

Hopefully as we mature as an adult, we can see that the stage of independence had its uses in our growth. It has helped us survive but it will no longer serve us as our primary lens on life. In a state of independence, we are looking at the world like a mouse scurrying in the undergrowth of life. Everything is in close-up and it's impossible to get a perspective on the bigger picture.

But when we move into the interdependence stage of development we rise above the undergrowth and have a vision like that of an eagle soaring over the landscape. When we view life through this lens of interdependence, we realise that we are an integral part of the living organism that is planet Earth. At the interdependent stage of development we become aware that our actions, and even our thoughts and feelings have influence on those around us and on the environment. Irrespective of our status, wealth or health, the reality is that we are all interdependent. It is a vast and cosmic view of life, and it has huge implications for us as we grow older.

Of course, you don't have to be in the second half of life to understand holistic theory. Particle physicists and biologists are fully aware of the interconnectedness of life. Young and old are becoming increasingly awake to the fact that all human life is interdependent with nature. With more people on the planet chasing fewer resources, we have a growing awareness of the connection between ourselves and nature. Ironically, the ecological crisis has helped us see that all species are ultimately dependent on other species and the environment. By crossing the barriers between different disciplines, scientists increasingly understanding that we live in a world of interconnected, complex networks.

Nature lays down layer upon layer of ever greater complexity and connection. Atoms come together to create molecules which in turn come together to form macromolecules such as DNA. DNA combines to create organelles which unite to create cells. The cells join to create tissue which links up to create the organs in our body upon which we are dependent.

While we might understand this holistic view of life with our mind, there is an exciting opportunity as we grow older to embrace the interconnectedness of all life with our very being. In a way this is like joining up all the fragmented pieces of our existence and by doing this we can start to experience the inner power of our whole being. Instead of us feeling separate from the world, we sense that we are an integral part of it. Instead of having an objective view of the world with life and death being part of a static and closed structure, we can open ourselves up to the mystery and wonder of our inner power. As the American psychologist Erik H. Erikson said, Life doesn't make any sense without interdependence. We need each other, and the sooner we learn that, the better for us all.

CARRIE'S STORY: A wake-up call

Twenty years ago, Carrie and her partner Tom adopted a boy with mental health issues. Bringing up Nathan was challenging but they were both committed parents. They fought many battles until by the time Nathan turned twenty-four, he had developed a degree of independence. One morning a couple of months after Nathan went into supported accommodation, Tom announced that he had prostate cancer. Carrie took some deep breaths. They had been through so much together. She started thinking through all possibilities including a funeral. The weeks went by. There were tests and more tests. And then as the months passed the drama subsided and they were told Tom might live for another thirty years.

Some strange emotions went through Carrie. Of course, she was relieved but then she felt some resentment and anger. It wasn't completely directed at Tom but she started to question whether she loved him. And then she did something completely out of character. She booked a walking holiday in Scotland on her own. This was unprecedented. She just knew she needed to do it. She needed to be alone and re-think everything. She says it was something about the preciousness of life that she had been missing. It was the start of a new journey for Carrie.

ARRESTED DEVELOPMENT

Fearing old age and death prevents further development and leads to isolation

It is notoriously difficult to move on from being an independently-minded individual to a mature, holistic adult in our culture. It requires an acceptance of our vulnerability and the transience of life. It is impossible to develop a deep sense of interconnection if we unable to acknowledge the basic laws of nature. We cannot gain the eagle's view on life if we are avoiding the reality of ageing and death. If we can't accept the second law of thermodynamics that states that there is a natural tendency of any isolated system to degenerate into a more disordered state, then we are doomed to scurry around like the lone mouse in the undergrowth of life.

The Pressure to Stay Young

Why is it so difficult to accept our ageing? We see the process working in all creatures without exception.

We see the seasons changing and know that all plants and trees grow old and die. Yet, most of us have some fundamental concerns about growing older. In the Life-Stage workshops participants were asked what concerns they had about growing older. These were five of the most common responses;

- Loss of physical and mental abilities
- Fear of the dying process
- Loss of family and friends.
- Loneliness and isolation
- Not having enough resources in old age.

Anxiety might seem like a natural response to ageing from a human being who has developed a degree of self-awareness that is not seen in the rest of the animal kingdom. Of course, we don't want to see our capabilities diminishing or to lose family and friends. We want to stay young and relevant for as long as possible. When that's not credible any more, we want to stay middle-aged for as long as possible. We may want to keep up with the generations younger than us so that we don't become invisible. But our development in the second half of life won't progress if we succumb to the external pressure to prize youthfulness over our well-being.

Youth has always been desired and envied. There is an endless fascination with newness and its potential while tedium and predictability is often associated with the old. It's a harsh truth that most people are spontaneously affectionate to a puppy, but an arthritic, old dog probably doesn't get the same attention. The media in particular love youth with its skin-elasticity, flexibility, energy and sex appeal. Youth is pleasing to the eye and advertisers know that the beauty and energy of youth sells products to customers. The reckless daring of the young creates excitement and drama for the media and the entertainment industry. The fittest and the best are cheered on by millions at major sporting events with the vast majority of competitors being in their 20s. In a youth-orientated culture, ageing is generally seen as a negative, and opinions expressed in the media around older people are often derogatory. The stereotypical language used to describe an older person might include 'over the hill', 'incompetent', 'sad', 'asexual' or 'needy'. So, it is not surprising that there is considerable pressure on us to keep looking, thinking and feeling as young as possible.

Our vulnerability to the cultural imperative to stay young provides a huge business opportunity to the cosmetic industry. As we age, the skin becomes thinner and blood vessels become visible. The reality of ageing includes wrinkles, sagging skin, age spots, freckles and changes to pigmentation caused by sunlight. There's a vast array of potions and lotions to keep the skin looking fresh and elastic, and if that's not enough, there's botox

40
YEARS
OLD
IT'S PROBABLY TIME TO
START LYING ABOUT YOUR AGE

50
is
the
new
40.*
*said no one ever
happy birthday old-timer

60-YEAR-OLD
XING
WRINKLE WAY
VIAGARA FALLS
MEMORY MEMORIAL

69
UNTIL FURTHER NOTICE

and then, when push comes to shove, there's always cosmetic surgery. The cosmetic surgery industry[16] in the UK is currently worth around £3.6 billion and growing. Fillers and other surgical procedures are becoming the new norm if you can afford them. As an advertiser's slogan goes; 'it's your face, your choice – right?' Surgical and even non-surgical work carry some physical risk and a greater psychological risk, but in an image-conscious society, women of all ages and a growing number of men think it's a risk worth taking. The 'grey tsunami' is a huge sales opportunity for the cosmetics industry, but their marketing depends on maintaining the myth that you need to look young to be happy.

Social media has helped a bandwagon of anti-ageing gurus promote products and services designed to keep us looking and feeling younger. In the era of the selfie, looking good is closely associated with feeling good. The positive ageing movement is thriving and appealing to baby-boomers to 'live life to the full'. Magazines that target an older readership use images of younger-looking models who are "ageing successfully".

Advertisers hint at a happy and affluent lifestyle for older generations. There is the smiling and kind grandparent with child on the knee, or the distinguished mentor figure dispensing some wisdom. A woman surfing in her 70s is held up as an inspiring role model. The message is that that we, too, can achieve incredible things if we try hard. Of course, we want to be making the most of our lives. Who wants to be a lonely, old woman asleep in an armchair when you could be out catching some big waves? Or shuffling around a potting shed when you could be running marathons? Avoiding such stereotypes of ageing can be a seductive message for those of us in the second half of life, but it can also put a pressure on us to perform and keep up appearances. We are getting a barrage of images and messages that tell us that getting old is negative and death is unacceptable.

Yes, of course, we want to stay fit and active for as long as we can, but our well-being in the second half of life is much more complex than staying fit and active. We need emotional and spiritual development as we age as much as physical activity. It's not so much about accomplishments and running marathons although the positive ageing adverts would like us to think so. We can't access our inner power if we are over-concerned with superficial looks and achievements. If we are pre-occupied with appearances and a bucket list of things to achieve, we may miss hearing the call.

Hearing the Call

In the complex world of independence and separation, it's easy to miss the invitation. It's easy to mistake the message and think that Nature is telling you that you're not as skinny as you used to be, and you need to go on a diet, or you need to find a new and younger partner. The call often comes at a time when there's a change of role or identity such as children leaving home. The empty nest may make you question your identity as a parent, but may also encourage you to look a little deeper, now that the hurly-burly of bringing up children is over. A change in the business or work, including redundancy or retirement, can trigger a deeper enquiry into your values. An illness or an operation might also lead to a questioning of life's meaning.

Different psychological stressors come into play as we deal with change in the autumn of our days. While some say that there is no such thing as a mid-life crisis, there would certainly appear to be a particular kind of phenomenon that happens to people somewhere between 45 and 65. It could be the death of a relative or a friend or some other shock that makes us consider what lies behind the facade and the labels. It is entirely natural that the independent-thinking adult who has survived the onslaught of adulthood now finds there is a lack of fulfilment and meaning. Sometimes this is manifested in a 'dark night of the soul', and at 3 am we go to an unfamiliar place inside of ourselves that we have never been to before.

The reptilian part of our brain and our ego has schemed and worked for our survival. They have done a great job in keeping us alive, but the ego now knows that it is fighting a losing battle. Such 'visitations' in the small hours could have been the wake-up call. The jolt that you needed to change. But by 9am. you've had a cup of coffee and you're not so sure. Things always look bleak at night. It's when the shadows come out to play. But now in the morning light things don't look so bad. Perhaps if you worked harder or were more disciplined things would be better. But for now, you can muddle through.

And maybe there was no crisis or dark night of the soul. Things ran smoothly for you in your 40s and 50s. Perhaps you have achieved a certain measure of power and success. The seeds that you sowed in the earlier part of your life had produced a harvest of abundance. People regard you as one of life's victors. You cruise through your 60s sampling the best of all that the modern world has to offer. But somewhere down the line there is a growing awareness that something is missing. You're aware that total fulfilment has not been reached, and that deep inside of you there is a longing for something. The trouble is that the mind can't quite describe it and you can't buy it on Amazon.

And what of those of us who don't feel the power of success in mid-life? Those of us that have just managed to survive. We, who have struggled in the mundane world with fear and sadness, and moments of joy and hope? We too reach this place of gradual awareness. Without the distraction of wealth or fame, perhaps we become aware of the mystery of nature more easily than those high-flying achievers.

But still, there is that instinctive awareness for many of us that something is missing. A process. A ritual. A journey. How do I get to the end of my life with grace or at least with a modicum of self- respect? Surely this drifting gradually into old age and death isn't all that there is? Our intuition tells us there is something else. And there is more, but we frequently interpret this instinct the wrong way. It is not more material possessions, travel, sex or relationships. It's not more comfort and security or even more life. It is not more of anything. If we are at all conscious, we reach this place of awareness at some time in the second half of life. Regardless of gender. Whether rich or poor. Whether highly educated or not, it is on our developmental map. To stay in the stage of independence will not ultimately serve us. There is part of us that instinctively knows we need to move on. There is a transition that needs to happen. What our instinct is telling us is that we need to embrace both life and death in its fullness.

Looking for Answers

Some might look to science to provide answers to life, ageing and death, but while it can give detailed information about the ageing process, science doesn't have an easy to follow instruction manual on coming to terms with mortality. There are no answers to the big questions such as how life or the universe started. For every question that science answers many more are created. As the philosopher Mary Midgley[17] observed, 'Physical science is a tiny part of our view of the world'. Science can create a sense of wonder in us which as we will see later is an important tool in developing our power. It can point to the interconnectivity of all life, but it has no easy answers.

Religious communities offer a strong belief system to support people in coming to terms with their mortality. Traditionally, priests, rabbis and imams offer comfort to the older members of their congregation and offered a path to salvation through faith. But today we live in a secular world where nearly 50% of us have no affiliation to a religious community[18].

Putting it off

Because there are no ready-made answers, it is easy to drift unconsciously into old age. It is natural to procrastinate, to put off any thoughts of ageing and mortality and seek what morsels of security and comfort we can in day-to-day living. The scope of life can soon diminish and the older we get the harder it can be to change. If we don't heed the call to the next stage of development, then we may adopt unhelpful coping mechanisms to avoid anxiety about ageing and death. We may well hide and repress any anxiety and force it from consciousness. This denial and repression of feelings can lead to dysfunctional behaviour, regression and isolation.

When we were young it seemed as though we had an eternity to sort stuff out, but in the second half of life we become aware of the need to move on. The mind and the body may have dropped a few hints. There are strong reasons to go on a journey of transition and rise up above competitive individualism and self-interest and get a much wider view that incorporates both life and death. Rather than pull up the duvet and pretend that we're not getting any older, we can use our inner power to enjoy the present moment and our old age. Now we know that our time is limited, we can take up the challenge to live with meaningful connection and purpose.

BETTINA'S STORY – Death enabled a new start

When she was six or seven, her daughter used to ask about her childhood, but Bettina never wanted to talk about her upbringing. Bettina's past was a closed book. There was little family connection of any type other than the occasional birthday card. Bettina saw her daughter becoming more engaged in her own life until she only came back to the flat to eat and sleep. When Bettina heard that her estranged father was in a hospice, she went to visit him not because of love or duty but out of a sense of curiosity. She couldn't imagine her father being vulnerable, so despite some trepidation she went to the hospice to visit him. The best she could say about him was that he was a cold man.

He recognized her but didn't say anything and then fell asleep. She sat there by his bedside with the staff going about their business. A nurse told her about her father's diagnosis while Bettina felt numb. She sat there for a long time by his bedside while all around her was a sense of calm and caring. Before the visiting hours were up one of the cleaners who was a woman of her own age made a cup of tea for Bettina.

One evening about six months after her father died, Bettina was on her second glass of wine when she felt something approaching disgust at her life. But she didn't have a third glass of wine. She kept thinking about her time at the hospice and the people who worked there. And the woman who made her a cup of tea. The next day Bettina didn't go to the council offices where she worked, but went to the hospice to find out how she could become a volunteer. She felt that this would be a good place to start a new life.

THE TRANSITION

Moving on from a confined worldview is challenging, but is necessary to access power

It's hard to change. Much easier to stay youngish and independently-minded. Moving from one stage of life to another is no easy task, but throughout human history there is a long tradition of ritualising[19] the transition. In many indigenous cultures, it is marked by a rites of passage ceremony where initiates detach from their old life and identity before entering into a sacred or liminal space where they are prepared for their new roles in the community. For example, teenage boys in the Maasai tribe of East Africa go through a grueling ordeal before they can be accepted by the community as an adult. The process can be often terrifying and has been seen as barbaric by some western anthropologists. But within the tribe the process was seen as absolutely necessary for the communal well-being. The five major African initiation rites are birth, adulthood, marriage, eldership and ancestorship. These are seen as fundamental for human growth and development. According to Professor Manu Ampim[20];

> 'These rites were originally established by African ancestors while they were living in order to link the individual to the community and the community to the broader and more potent spiritual world.'

The rites of passage ritual made the initiate confront their deepest fears and leave their past identity behind. Traditionally, in the ceremony an initiate goes through a threshold or a portal from the mundane world into what is called liminal space where conventional time and space have little meaning. It is seen as sacred and the place where a profound change of consciousness takes place. Once the initiate was through the threshold, the initiate would leave behind the limited mind and connect to the spirit world and their ancestors. After the ritual, the initiate was welcomed back into their community with their new identity.

For much of our lives we've been assiduously building our identity. Our personality. Our character. It is who we are, so for most of us leaving behind our old identity is terrifying. To lose our sense of independence which we have worked so hard for is as alarming as a young man of the Vanuartu tribe undergoing a landing diving initiation[21]. In indigenous societies there is a fundamental distinction made between an "elder" and an "older" person. The elders main function was to guard the stories and the values of the tribe. Today we have no tribe. We have lost the lineage hundreds of generations ago. Our stories and values come from multiple cultures and we have no rites of passage.

We have many 'olders' who wonder what is going on but no initiated elders.

In the west our various religions have provided such markers as baptism, aqiqah, catechism and bar mitzvah, but we live in an increasingly secular world where we celebrate more than initiate. The journey into adulthood might be marked by graduation or the first pay cheque. Marriage or partnership is often ritualised within the community but from then on, there is little to mark the stages of life except for a bus pass and a pension until, finally, the ritual of our funeral.

The transition into a mature adult involves coming out of a state of illusion that we are somehow separate. It's about embracing the inter-connection of all things with not just our minds but with our actions and behaviour, rising up above competitive individualism and self-interest to get a much wider view of life.

There are people of different generations all over the world seeking a shift in their consciousness. Some try drugs such as ayahuasca to find out who they are, or spend days alone in the desert on a vision quest. Others work with gurus who might offer signposts to a more meaningful existence. Retreats may start you on your journey and spiritual practices such as yoga and meditation can support you, but ultimately nothing outside yourself will give you direct access to your inner power. To ask fundamental questions about our identity and life choices takes a willingness to be vulnerable and involves a degree of surrender as well as an acceptance that our minds are limited. A change in consciousness can't be brought about just through the rational mind. It requires another part of us (that some call the soul) to see that we are no longer alone and disconnected. We are part of an organism. We may know this intellectually, but it is not until we have deeper connection with the great mystery of life and death that we can make the transition.

Facing the Journey

In many of the best fairy tales the hero or heroine has to go on a long journey to discover the treasure and after much hardship and travelling will come to a place where they are severely tested. In the Russian fairy tales[22], it is often the witch Baba Yaga who challenges the protagonist. There, in the middle of the vast forest is the grotesque old woman who represents a powerful force of nature. It is only by confronting this unpleasant aspect of life can the heroine find her way to happiness. In the legend of

King Arthur, it is Parzival[23] who comes up against the hideous witch Cundrie. She seems cruel and malevolent and only there to shame and humiliate Parzival. But it is only through his confrontation with Cundrie that Parzival can finally find the Holy Grail. Again, Cundrie represents the powerful force of Nature that challenges the hero on a deep level. Despite looking like an adversary, Cundrie is there to ensure that Parzival finds not superficial flattery but his true inner power. This journey of transition is a common theme in legends, myths, stories and films. In The Hero with a Thousand Faces, Joseph Campbell[24] details the psychological forces in the passage of transition and famously inspired the director, George Lucas, in the making of the Star Wars films.

And so it is with ageing. No matter how great our triumphs and achievements, no matter our status or character, we come to a point in the second half of life where we have an option to look deeply at our vulnerability and go on our journey with courage, wisdom and love. Or to live in denial, fear or some vain hope that we will be alright.

We may think we could never be like Parzival or Vasilisa who goes alone into the forest to confront the Baba Yaga. We may even dismiss such folklore as irrelevant, or too esoteric for us. But we can become existential heroes by acknowledging our vulnerability. We, too, are on a precarious journey. In the stories and myths, it is in the darkest place that the protagonist discovers inner qualities that they didn't know they possessed. It seems a universal law of nature that if we accept the challenge of transition, then the latent forces of the universe become manifest and support us on our journey. Without undergoing the journey, our inner power will remain latent because it is not needed. It's a tragedy that many people die unfulfilled or feeling that they have missed something in life. At some point the challenge of ageing needs to be met full on so that we can extract all the power that is inherent in our lives. Just like those vulnerable heroes and heroines of myth and folklore!

JACKIE'S STORY: A close call with Death

Jackie says the heart attack was a blessing. She was an HR manager at a University where there seemed to be a constant series of employment tribunal cases in progress. Some of the disputes had become ugly and the toxic atmosphere became increasingly stressful for Jackie. At home she was always trying to keep the peace … until the day she collapsed on the pavement four doors up from her own house. She was lucky to survive, and the doctor encouraged her to think about all aspects of her lifestyle. Jackie felt some shame about collapsing on the pavement. It felt like she had let everyone down.

In her recovery time she started to explore how she could change, and one weekend made a very clear intention to 'find her calling' as she put it. It started with watercolours and quickly moved to acrylics before jumping into oils. The canvases became larger and larger and she sold a few of them. Her old peer group thought her artistic journey eccentric, but she didn't care anymore what people thought. She made new friends and had a couple of exhibitions. She didn't sell much, but she had stopped worrying about money. After the heart attack she was living day to day and most days she experienced a sense of freedom and joy that she had not known before.

TRAVELLING LIGHT

Preparing for the journey by acknowledging loss

In earlier chapters we looked at the first of the four key elements in accessing our inner power – an interdependent perspective on life.

- an inter-dependent perspective on life
- our present breath
- our final breath
- our life intention

The next stage of the journey cannot be undertaken while multi-tasking or with a hectic mind. It requires a slowing down so that we can open ourselves up to transformation. The challenge is to find space and time within your own environment. For most of us, to find peace-of-mind and that sweet spot of stillness takes some self-discipline. Often our minds are working over-time to keep up with the rapid pace of daily life which prevents us from accessing our inner power.

There is no necessity to cut ourselves off from the world or from daily life. Our inner power is not best discovered in some remote or idyllic place, though most people find that some access to nature is important. Adjusting our schedule a little can give us time to come into the present. Do we need all the appointments and is all of the screen-time really necessary to our well-being? A conscious choice to give ourselves some breathing space is a good place to start this journey. It may be meditation, yoga or a spiritual practice that helps you into the present. It may be sitting in nature or simply being conscious of your breathing. If we enter a space where we can be conscious of any distractions without needing to react to them, then we come into the present which is where we need to be, in order to start the journey.

We are here in the present moment with decades of experiences inside of us. Within us are memories of significant moments; failures, successes, pains and pleasures. We probably have at least twice as many memories inside us as when we became an adult. Some of what we carry around from the past may be good and some of it may be weighing us down like a heavy rucksack that we carry around everywhere. This is a good opportunity to unpack or at least recognize some of the baggage that is not essential for the onward journey. Even if we could unpack everything, there is no need to do so. Just by acknowledging what we carry can help lighten the load. We can start by checking-in with ourselves around what we have lost.

Loss and Grief

By the time that we get to our fifth decade, most of us will have known plenty of loss. The loss of relatives. The loss of youth and friendships. The loss of opportunities. The loss of pets. Even the loss of hair, teeth or 20/20 vision. As we go through the decades it is inevitable that our losses increase. Where we have a connection to an aspect of the living, there is inevitable loss. Grief is the natural response to loss and an emotion that is woven into the fabric of life. By opening ourselves up to grief we can liberate ourselves and re-connect with our humanity.

Grief is worrying to an independently-minded individual, and is often seen as something negative or unpleasant. For many there's a discomfort around grief. Grief is seen as something that needs to be fixed as quickly as possible or it may be interpreted as a kind of failure. Grief is not a sign of weakness nor is it a lack of hope. Grief is an act of love for the world and for all life. We are helpless in the face of grief, but this is not a bad thing. It's an act of surrender not to anyone but to life itself. It is a purification of the heart.

When we were young, we were encouraged to grow out of shedding tears and crying as it showed a vulnerability that was not welcomed in main-stream culture unless it was for something specific like the death of a friend or relative. Even at a funeral, mourners might speak of how 'bravely' the bereaved widow behaved because she showed little of her deep emotion.

Since Elizabeth Kubler-Ross [25] wrote her book 'The Five Stages of Grief' in 1969, many books have been written and much academic research undertaken into the subject. It's a complicated picture with many theories and no quick-fix solutions. Of course, grief in some cases can lead to chronic dysfunction and may require specialist counselling. But, finding a healthy way to acknowledge our loss and the grief can be healing in the present and can enable us to celebrate the joy of living more fully. Grief and joy are human emotions that are profoundly connected. Relationships are given power and depth because consciously or unconsciously we know they are finite. The joy that comes from a beautiful connection with another living being, deepens our grief when we lose that relationship.

To ignore our losses will not help us lead a healthy life as we grow older. At this stage in our journey we cannot waste our valuable energy denying our true feelings. Grief contains the seeds of compassion, wisdom and courage so that in the late afternoon of life we can count our losses as well as our blessings. Grief can be like a medicine and by shying away from grief, we keep our lives small. To live fully we need to be in touch with our grief and not hide from it.

> ### EXERCISE 2 – Invitation To Explore Loss
>
> The invitation is to think of three losses in your life. They do not have to be the biggest or the most dramatic. It could be the death of someone, the loss of a relationship or loss of anything that meant something to you. Spend a little time thinking about each of the three losses and how you feel about them. When you are ready, write about each loss in your journal. The entry maybe a couple of sentences or several paragraphs.

The storing up of loss and grief without having a healthy outlet can lead to the stereotypical image of an older person as someone who complains all the time - the stock cartoon figure of the grumbling old age pensioner who moans about their aches and pains. This stereotype tells whoever will listen about the terrible state of the world and how it wasn't like that in their day. They live in the past and see their ailments as an unjust punishment, or they blame them on incompetent doctors. The music is too loud and the children are rude. It's their partner's fault and the neighbours are to blame. Acknowledging our grief can free us from the stereotype.

HELEN'S STORY: Forgotten grief

Some would say that Helen lived a very privileged life. She was active in her community, though was seen as a little detached and aloof. On a well-being retreat at the age of 58, she was invited to participate in a grief circle. At first Helen thought this a strange idea. No one close to her had died recently. She was generally happy with her life and grief was not something she wished to be involved with. But she went along with her friend.

There were around a dozen of them in a circle near an old oak tree in the woods. The facilitator invited them to step in and form an inner circle if they had a parent who had died. She watched from the outer circle as some on the inner circle named their dead parents. Helen felt awkward watching these people open up to their grief. When the facilitator invited anyone in the outer circle who had a close friend die, Helen stayed where she was. And then it hit her; one of her best friends, Elise, had drowned in Greece when she was on holiday with her parents. But that was when they were both teenagers. Helen stepped into the inner circle and spoke her friend's name for the first time in over thirty years. She thought she had dealt with her emotions around this tragedy but under the huge oak tree she felt the grief coming to the surface. She felt safe enough to allow her feelings to emerge completely as she started sobbing. And then her grief seemed to embrace the pain and loss of so much more than just her friend. When Helen had finished weeping her tears, she felt exhausted but also a wonderful calm and sense peace came over her. She started to wonder about all the grief people had buried in their hearts and never let go of. This episode had a powerful effect on the next stage of Helen's life.

SAM'S STORY: Dealing with grief

After his mother's death Sam got a call from an old friend, Peter, who suggested he buy a book called The Grief Recovery Method. Sam didn't think he was particularly grief stricken or that he needed rescuing. But he bought the book out of curiosity and respect for his friend. After some discussion they set up a safe space each week to work through one of the chapters. In the hour-long sessions, they were both surprised at the depth of the work. Sam would speak of his feelings while Peter listened attentively and then they swapped over. They shared their emotions

> and vulnerability together and occasionally needed the tissues from the box that was strategically placed between them. With the help of the book, Sam created an emotional timeline of his history with his mother and wrote a letter to her. It was a powerful experience that helped Sam to both forgive his mother and his feel gratitude to her. Sam realized he could have easily missed this opportunity if it hadn't been for his friend's invitation.

Gratitude

Of course, growing old has many challenges as we discussed earlier, but how we respond to them is key. If we externalize responsibility for our happiness, we risk ending up a sad and helpless victim. If we think that life has treated us unfairly, then we will inevitably struggle to be fulfilled or happy. It is easy to be irritable as we lose flexibility or as our eyesight or hearing deteriorates. We could feel resentment as we see young people flaunt their flexibility and energy. We could feel jealous about how young people take their abilities that we once had, for granted. The antidote to this mindset is a conscious practice of appreciation for our life. For all that we are, and all that we have. This is hard to do if we are continuously trying to keep up with the pace of the independent individual. We need some space and time to breathe into a sense of gratitude.

Over the last couple of decades there has been much research that shows that grateful people are happier[26], less stressed and more satisfied with their lives and relationships. In several studies, gratitude is shown to help people sleep better and to contribute to their overall well-being.

Most spiritual practices and religions encourage an appreciation of life. It used to be common practice for Christians to say 'grace' before a meal which might go something like 'For what we are about to receive, may the Lord make us truly thankful.' This prayer can be a wonderful connection to a deep sense of gratitude, or it can be a meaningless formality. Gratitude for our food might involve an appreciation of the soil, the rain, the seasons and life itself. The food that keeps us alive can show us how interconnected we are to nature and other people. There may be a supply chain involving hundreds of people to bring a simple meal to our table. Whether our spiritual practice is prayer, chanting or simply walking in nature, gratitude also opens us up to a larger perspective to our place in the universe. As Joanna Macey[27] says; "Gratitude is liberating. It is subversive. It helps us realise that we are sufficient, and that realization frees us."

To be resentful, envious or jealous may be understandable but it is foolishness when seen from the inter-dependent view of life. An on-going practice of gratitude enables our inner wisdom and compassion to come to the forefront of our life.

EXERCISE 3 – Gratitude Invitation

The invitation is to write in your journal one thing for which you are grateful every day for a week. It might be a sentence or two or you might want to explore your appreciation for someone or something more deeply. This simple exercise can have a profound effect on your well-being.

THE GREAT MYSTERY

Opening up to the mystery enables great benefit

Once we have acknowledged some of our losses, and then taken the time to appreciate aspects of our life, we are ready to approach the threshold of the Great Mystery. It is within the Great Mystery that we can find the inner power to transform our grief into joyful connection and purpose.

As mentioned in Chapter 5 stepping through the threshold in a rites-of-passage ritual requires us to let go of our analytical mind in order to open ourselves up to a more powerful way of being in a new stage of our life. The mind has limitations and there is another essential part of our being that we need once we pass through the threshold.

The mind appears to be natures' most incredible creation as it handles perception, language and emotion. It can memorise, make judgements, choices and plans, but there are some things that the mind is unable to grasp. Our brain contains about 86 billion nerve cells[28] or neurons which are connected by trillions of connections, or synapses. Despite such awesome computing power, evolutionary psychologists suspect that there are aspects of nature and life such as free will and consciousness, that lie outside the limits of human thinking[29]. There are some fundamental mysteries that we may never solve. For example, we don't know how our universe came into being. Particle physicists have a mass of data about what happened a second after the 'big bang', but they don't know what went on a second before. Perhaps the universe has always existed or there are an infinite number of multi-verses. The truth is no one knows, and with every scientific break-through comes more questions. It is in our nature to want answers, so it is hard to accept that there may never be a unifying theory of consciousness and how the cosmos came into being? Whether it's cracking DNA coding, doing a sudoku puzzle or working out who did the crime, the human mind loves solving mysteries, but to access our inner power we need to acknowledge that the mind has limitations and that there is another part of us that we can utilise to help transform our lives as we get older.

The Complexity of Life

Our mind is used to working with the three dimensions of space (length, width and depth) and the one dimension of time but theoretical physicists say this is an artificial contruct (of the independent mind) and does not represent the nature of reality. The theory of general relativity maintains we live in a four-dimensional universe, and string theory says there are 10 dimensions while many mathematicians now propose that there of 24 dimensions. The cosmologist, Sean Carroll[30], maintains the universe evolves into a mathematical realm of 10,000 trillion, trillion, trillion, trillion, trillion, trillion, trillion, trillion dimensions. The mind cannot really conceive of such huge numbers but there is another part of us that has the potential to integrate with the vastness and the interconnectedness of all life. This part of us is outside of linear time and space which is why the mind has difficulty in identifying and labelling it. It is that part of us that connects to the mystery of life. Perhaps this simple graphic might put the knowledge that comes from the mind into perspective.

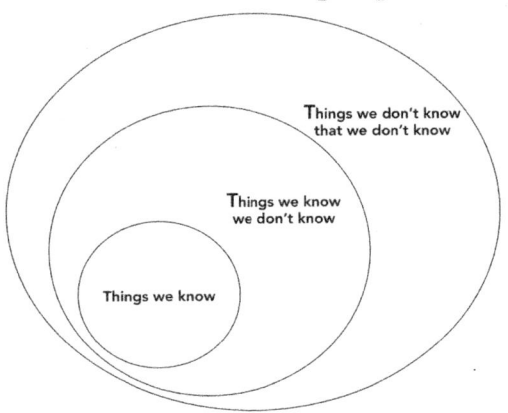

Definition Impossible

Different cultures and traditions use different terminology. For the Lakota tribe[31] the Great Mystery is not seen as a deity but as an encompassing life force and energy existing in all things. It is a great unifying force that flows in and through all things. Some might refer to the mystery as God while others might call it Qi or fundamental 'life force'. On the Twelve Step programmes, addicts talk about the 'Higher Power'. Whatever we choose to call this energy, it is notoriously hard to define. We can only use the language of our minds which falls short in the face of such a challenge. It is outside of our understanding of time and space.

The Soul

There's a part of our being which some call the soul or the spirit that connects to the Great Mystery. This is the part of our being that is not concerned with separation, independence, boundaries, and how much we have in our bank account. The soul (or whatever you chose to call it) is not so concerned with our individual survival in the mundane world, but it plays a vital part in our moment by moment happiness as we grow older. It exists in everyone but while we are in the dependent and independent stage of life, it may well be dormant for much of the time. The soul might put in a strong appearance at the birth of a baby or at the death of a loved one. The soul is undefinable and unqualifiable and is best described by poets such as Rumi[32] or Rainer Maria Rilke[33]. The famous lines below from William Blake's poem, the Auguries of Innocence, do not make any logical sense and yet we instinctively know that they contain a deeper truth. They connect to the soul.

> To see a World in a Grain of Sand
> And a Heaven in a Wild Flower
> Hold Infinity in the palm of your hand
> And Eternity in an hour

As the part of us that connects to the great mystery, the soul has limitless potential to affect how we are in the second half of life. As we grow older our physical energy diminishes and our capabilities may become limited, but we can more than compensate by developing this connection to the great mystery. Some say the soul is the most sacred part of a person and is communicated through love. It is through the soul and its connection to the great mystery that we can gain a holist perspective on life and death.

A deep awareness of the soul in us may come about in many ways. It may be through spiritual practice or through profound experiences in nature. Some have accessed this part of themselves through great challenges or through severe illness. For us in the second half of life the opportunity to access the inner power through our soul's connection with the great mystery, lies in acceptance of the transience of life. By opening ourselves up to this mystery and the wonder of life and death, we can access our inner power.

EXERCISE 4 – Recognising The Soul

What does 'soul' mean to you? Is it more than just a genre of music? In your journal write some words about glimpsing your soul. You might be aware of this part of yourself when watching a sunset or listening to the wind in the trees. Other signs your dormant soul is stirring might include feeling unusually restless – none of your usual pursuits cut it, or you want something, but you don't know what – you can't put a name to it.

JACK'S STORY: Re-discovering the Mystery

In 2020, Jack had to cancel the family holiday to Greece due to the Covid epidemic and quarantine regulations. The family went camping instead and on the first night of the trip, Jack couldn't sleep as he lay in the tent worrying about his job.

As it was getting light at 4.30am, Jack got out of his sleeping bag and started to walk from the camp site and down a nearby nature trail. He would be 50 next week and it didn't feel good. He was anxious about his daughters' education. He was uneasy about his marriage? His mum was not well. He was fearful for the future.

As the dawn started to break, Jack followed the path into a wood and walked for a while until he came to a clearing. He sat on a log feeling empty and alone. He was close to tears as he searched his tired brain for some kind of a solution to his life.

Jack sat there as the sunlight started to come through the trees and he became aware of the bird song all around him. After an hour or so, it became obvious to Jack that he was not alone. There was life all around him and despite his problems, the almost-fifty-year-old remembered how as a child he had built a camp in the woods with his friend.

> As Jack slowly walked back to the site, he was full of wonder at the beauty of the leaves on the trees and mystery of nature. He was really looking forward to rest of the holiday.

THE FEAR OF DEATH

Overcoming the fight, flight or freeze response mechanism

The only two absolute certainties in life are this present moment and our final breath. Everything else is speculation. Tomorrow may or may not happen, but this breath now and our final breath are inevitable. Can we influence how we leave the world of the living or are we powerless in the hands of fate? Surely too many random events happen in life for us to have any certainty?

In fact, from a holist or cosmic perspective these two moments are inextricably linked. What we feel in this moment affects our final moment. If the present moment is full of anger or sadness, then the final breath is likely to contain some of that emotional energy. If we have gratitude in this moment, it will manifest in some form at our dying time. Thus, we do have the power to influence our passing.

Once we have slowed down and acknowledged any grief we are carrying, we can take the next step towards accessing our power. This involves looking at the fundamental fear of ageing and being fully conscious of our mortality.

The Practice of Death

Throughout history, cultures have known how potent an awareness of death can be. Socrates encouraged his students to practice the art of dying. In ancient Japan there was a code of ethics for the fierce Samurai warriors[34] that read;

> "...morning after morning, the practice of death, considering whether it will be here or be there, imagining the most sightly way of dying, and putting one's mind firmly in death. Although this may be a most difficult thing, if one will do it, it can be done. There is nothing that one should suppose cannot be done"

In earlier days Christians would remind themselves of their mortality with memento mori[35] – literally, reminders of death. Artists would be paid by their wealthy patrons to heighten their awareness of the transience of life with skulls and images of decay in their paintings.

Today, for many people life is so busy that they get little time to consider their mortality. The consumer society has the power to distract us from such vital issues as ageing and death. There are endless virtual entertainments that might prevent us from looking at the reality of our existence. But as we get older the health of relatives and friends starts to deteriorate and it becomes harder to ignore the fact that we have limited time on this earth.

"In a busy train station in China commuters watch on as a passing monk says prayers for a man who has died."

In today's secular world the reality of death is pushed to the edge of our society so that we don't have to think about it. End-of-life care and funerals are professionalised so that family and friends don't need to be involved in the processes. The large, extended family has been in decline and with the rise of the nuclear family, inter-generational connections have weakened. There are nearly half a million people in UK care homes[36] and that number is rising. It is considered sensible by many to shield young people from the reality of old age and death as much as possible as 'it might be upsetting for them'. But the life force of both the young and the old is weakened if we hide from our mortality. In the UK, we have much to thank the NHS for, but we cannot rely on the state to make our ageing and end-of-life as good as it should be. The doctors can negate or manage the physical pain and they can sedate us so that we don't feel the angst and terror of ageing and death. In fact, they can take all of our feelings and power away so that we are oblivious to everything. As Woody Allen said, 'I don't mind dying ... as long as I don't have to be there when it happens.' This sums up what many people today feel – they don't want to be there at the end.

There are many superstitions around death and there is a kind of taboo in talking about death in polite society as though it might bring about some tragedy. It is seen as depressing or even fatalistic to talk about the end of life. But talking openly and discussing our fears and feelings around death can be surprisingly liberating. As a species we have an inherent need to share and communicate, yet the most profound event that we will experience is ignored!

Death Cafes

In 2011 Jon Underwood started the Death Café[37] movement where people drink tea, eat cake and discuss death. To date there have been over 11,000 Death Cafés all over the world. Their stated aim is to increase awareness of death to help people make the most of their finite lives. Although people may be strangers and from very different walks of life, there is no shortage of things to talk about. Far from being a depressing experience, a Death Café generally leaves people feeling invigorated. There is humour, vulnerability and honest connection.

While Jon himself died suddenly in 2017, his enormous influence on death cultures lives on. His thinking still encourages many to consider death – and life – in more vital and innovative ways.

RITA'S STORY: Reconnecting after grief

The two of them had some golden years but after Philip died, Rita felt very much on her own. Without her other half there seemed little point. She had given her all to Philip and now there was nothing left. Her family and friends tried to engage her in conversation and activities but Rita withdrew from life. Despite some counselling, she felt abandoned and alone.

Her oldest friend, Leah, finally persuaded Rita to meet at a local cafe. After some small talk, Leah told Rita she wanted her to come to choir practice. Leah went on and on about how Rita would love the conductor who was a genius and really funny. And how they all went for a drink together afterwards. 'Just try it out once', pleaded Leah. 'You'll love it.' Rita listened to her friend with disinterest and told her she was not going to go and that was that. After her gushing enthusiasm, Leah felt deflated by her friend's rejection. On the wall of the café she noticed a small poster. 'What on earth is a death café?' Rita looked at the poster with an illustration of a teapot and a slice of cake. 'We could go together', Leah said hopefully.

When Leah and Rita went a couple of days later, there were ten people drinking tea, eating cake and talking about death. They were a mixed bunch. Not Rita's type of people at all. She didn't really join in the conversations but the following month

> Rita looked forward to going with Leah as she felt she had something to offer. Here her brio and her enthusiasm for life could find a new outlet, and she added a questing, fearless dimension to discussions about death that many participants found valuable.

Coming to Terms with Mortality

Albert Camus, the atheist and philosopher wrote; "Come to terms with death, thereafter anything is possible." How we see our own death may well be shaped by experiences of being with someone as they died. Perhaps a friend or a relative. It may have been peaceful or traumatic, but there were probably some profound moments for you. Death can be a beautiful experience for some and a torment for others. Some die with acceptance and with gratitude for their life. Others may die in a state of terror filled with anger or regret.

So, considering our own death with a resolute mind is crucial if we are to transform the fear into meaningful connection and purpose. How can we change our anxieties into empowerment? How do we develop a healthy connection to the end of life and our dying breath? Whatever your experience of witnessing death, the empowering factor is to know how you would you like to die?

EXERCISE 5 Visualising your Death

In this exercise, you are invited to spend some quiet time imagining your perfect death. This exercise helps us get in touch with our mortality and is best done with a friend. It can be an incredibly powerful experience with long term benefits. Agree on a set time to reflect deeply on the question - it could be for ten minutes or for hours. Imagine that you can die in exactly the way that you want. How would it be? In a room? On a bed? What are the sheets and the pillowcases like? Who is with you? Or are you alone? What kind of day is it outside? Is a window open? Or perhaps you would rather die in nature. Under a willow tree by a river? Or on a tropical island with the setting sun. The choice is yours. Is music being played as you take your last breath? What sounds can you hear? A human voice or the birds singing? This is your big, and final, moment. How would you like it to be? Imagine your ideal death from every single aspect and in as much detail as possible, and write detailed notes about it. This helps to make your mortality more real. It is good, after that, to share all of your thoughts with the friend who can listen attentively, and without comment or judgement. When you have described your perfect death in detail, you listen as your friend speaks. It is a simple exercise, but it can be a life-changing experience.

Thinking Ahead

Some say it doesn't matter how you die. It's the end of the story and that is that, but as Atul Gawande[38] wrote, 'We all want to be the authors of our own stories, and in stories endings matter'.

So, what if there was an element of choice in how we die? As I mentioned earlier, in an interdependent universe where everything is connected, what we do in this present moment will affect the last moment of our life. Therefore, it is logical to think ahead and to calmly assess how far we may be able to influence our death.

One difficulty in coming to terms with death is the fact that we don't know when it will happen. Do we have months, years or decades left? We're not comfortable with the unknown and can easily go into a place of fear. How bad could dying be? How will I cope? It is easy to picture the worst. We could be hit by a bus and it's over in a flash. Or it could be a long and slow demise with a disease such as Alzheimer's. We don't know. But as we will see in the next couple of chapters, the Law of Attraction is an integral part of the Great Mystery. It is empowering to believe that we have a choice about how we feel in the present and final moments of life. We can also incorporate this very uncertainty into our death practice. The Tibetan master Dudjom Lingpa[39] said,

> Examine the births and deaths of other beings and reflect again and again on the unpredictability of your lifespan and the time of your death, and on the uncertainty of your own situation. Meditate on this until you have definitively integrated it with your mind ... The appearances of this life, including your surroundings and friends, are like last night's dream, and this life passes more swiftly than a flash of lightning in the sky.'

Coming to terms with the failure of our ego and previous survival mechanisms can be frightening. As we saw in Maslow's Hierarchy of Needs exercise in Chapter 2, we are entrenched in our needs, and any deep change in these may present quite a threat. Individuality with the illusion of self-sufficiency increases our fear of death. If our primary need is for comfort and security, then it's unlikely that the inner powers of courage and compassion are going to be activated. Once we accept that quality of life is far more important than quantity, we will be freeing ourselves from the burden of fear and moving towards discovering the gold.

This can be a dark time for us, but it can also be an awakening and the start of a new adventure. The Jungerian psychologist Sam Keen[40] wrote;

'Cultivating awareness of our death leads to disillusionment, loss of character armour and a conscious choice to abide in the face of terror. The existential hero who follows this way of self-analysis differs for the average person in knowing that they are obsessed. Instead of hiding in the illusions of character, they see their impotence and vulnerability. The disillusioned hero rejects the standardised heroics of mass culture in favour of cosmic heroism in which there is real joy ... and new forms of courage and endurance.'

Our last breath maybe tomorrow or in 50 years' time, but it doesn't matter. It's going to happen sometime and there are great psychological benefits to looking at the practicalities around our death. Planning for our end of life doesn't make death happen any quicker.

Increasing awareness of our death and the last breath is a key element in accessing the power of ageing. But no amount of research, great death dialogues or advance planning will, on its own, enable us to fully access our inner power. In the next chapter we consider the need to connect the present moment and our final breath with an energy that comes from a personal 'life intention'.

> ## EXERCISE 6 – Advance Plan
>
> Think about making an Advance Plan. The act of completing an advance plan can create a more positive approach to both living and dying and so empower the planner no matter what age they are. Here are some of the things that you might want to consider in your advance plan but there's more detailed information in the appendix at the back of the book. Here are some aspects to consider;
>
> - Who you want to speak for you if you can't speak for yourself.
> - Your views on organ donation.
> - What to do about your online presence – social media, accounts etc.
> - Your affairs – where important papers are kept – will, Lasting Power of Attorney, pension information and so on

You don't need to be elderly or have a terminal diagnosis to plan for your death. By accepting and taking responsibility for our ending, we can enhance our life and lessen anxiety. It's easy to put it off and think we will do it later, but the relief of making a few decisions now can feel surprisingly liberating and empowering. We have more power over where and when we die than most people realise. Death has become increasingly medicalised and professionalised, but we can say now what we want and what we don't want at the end of life. Our directives and wishes around end of life needn't cost anything and can be legally binding. There are endless options for a funeral and by expressing our wishes, it can be really helpful for family and friends at a difficult time if they know before-hand what kind of ceremony we would like. We don't necessarily need a funeral director. Anyone or no one can officiate.

There is much evidence which shows that people who have planned in advance for the end of their life spend less time in hospital, receive fewer intensive treatments and have a greater quality of life when they reach their final days. But many find thinking about, talking about and planning for death frightening, and so avoid making any decisions about their dying time. This affects not just the individual and their carers but also the wider community. Only 8% of us want to die in hospital but 55% end up dying there. 63% of us want to die at home yet only 20% of us have that wish come true. Close friends and family are often left with a lack of clarity about the dying person wishes which can cause anxiety and confusion at a difficult time. The act of completing an advance plan can create a more positive approach to both living and dying and so empower the planner no matter what age they are.

In her book *With the End in Mind,* Dr Kathryn Mannix takes us into the world of palliative care and shows there is little to fear and much to prepare for when it comes to death: "There are only two days with fewer than twenty-four hours in each lifetime, sitting like bookends astride our lives: One is celebrated every year, yet it is the other that makes us see living as precious."

SABRINA'S STORY: Making preparation

Jack was proud of his daughter's achievements. At forty-four Sabina had a successful accounting business with her partner and had just acquired one of the hottest digital media companies as a new client. But Jack was not so happy about her sporting activities. She had been surfing for a while but when Sabina went chasing some extreme waves in Portugal, Jack felt she was being irresponsible. She had two teenage children and he asked his daughter to reconsider her trip. It was a dangerous activity. What if something happened to her?

It was typical of Sabina to respond to her father's question with detailed research. She wrote down her directives for the end of her life and what her wishes were, should she no longer have mental capacity. She was very clear about what she did and didn't want to happen. She detailed all of the arrangements for her own funeral including the type of coffin and the songs she wanted playing. And then she re-drafted her will. It took her a few of days but she felt somehow liberated. Jack asked his daughter if she had a death wish. 'No', said Sabrina. 'But I'm going to die sometime and I'm not going to live in fear.'

THE SEED OF INTENTION

Connecting the energy between the present and last breath with 'Life Intention'

When we were young, we might have had dreams and ambitions but now after a few decades of life experience, we have an opportunity to re-focus on what matters most to us in life. We have probably set intentions in the past, but now may be the time to re-appraise them. Do our goals from our youth still serve us? How do we want to live our life now the storms of youth and middle age are behind us? We have looked at the present moment and acknowledged some of what we carry with us. We have looked at the future and the fear of death and recognised that the present breath and the final breath are the only two certainties in life. In this chapter we are going to work on creating a 'life intention' that links these dual certainties.

We don't know how the future is going to be. It may be challenging, or it may be like a walk in the woods on a gentle autumn afternoon. No one knows, but we can prepare ourselves for any eventuality by having clarity about our underlying values and what we want for ourselves and the world. With a some carefully chosen words, we can create a life intention that can give us access to our inner power when we need it.

In the first half of life we may have set goals, made New Year's determinations, created an intention to improve our love life and set ourselves financial or fitness targets. It was a way to focus on achieving positive outcomes in our life. It produced good results sometimes and we got what we wanted. At other times we fell short, but the chances were that by setting a goal or a target, we learnt something about ourselves, or we moved on in some way.

We may have worked for a company that had a mission statement and a set of company values. The corporate world is full of goals and targets. Not only do they give organisations impetus, they also enable them to measure performance. Bosses can evaluate what's working and what needs to be improved. Personal trainers and coaches also work to find out what your quantifiable goals are, and then help you to achieve them. Setting a target is a powerful motivator in personal development work, and it's not just about reaching the dreamed-of result or the final achievement, it's as much about maintaining focus and enjoying the journey.

The law of attraction[41]

Intention is the most powerful tool for creating the change that we want to see. The 'law of attraction' is a results-orientated phenomenon with a foundation in positive psychology, goal-achieving research, and mind-brain sciences. It states that like tends to attract like and positivity usually attracts positivity, and negativity usually attracts negativity. Such books as *The Secret* by Rhona Byrne have spawned an industry of self-help books which focus mainly on the materialistic or achievement aspects of the law of attraction. If we want money, for example, we have to believe we can get it. This belief will then work into our thoughts which will transfer into words so that we take the action to get the money we desire. The law of attraction is not a new idea nor is it a secret. Many of the workshops and self-help books are aimed at an audience who want to be rich, powerful or charismatic. They want to thrive as individuals in a disconnected world of independence. They use the power of visualisation and intention to gain the rewards. The gurus of the law of attraction talk about how the universe provides for you if you make a clear intention. But the law of attraction is much stronger if the connection with the universe is a two-way, inter-dependent relationship. In other words, when we create a 'life intention' that is about giving as well as receiving what we want, we can access phenomenal power. So, we need to be fully conscious about what we want for ourselves and others. In the second half of life we need to gain clarity about how we intend to be, rather than what we desire to achieve.

Setting a Life Intention

We may need to accomplish certain goals or tick off items from a bucket list, but a life intention goes beyond the independent aims of the individual. It is bigger than a one-off experience or achievement. This is not to undermine individual targets and specific determinations which may create value for us and others. They may energise and reward us, but a life intention creates an over-arching framework that can contain all of our wants and needs. There is no universal understanding of what words to use when we resolve to do something, but the table below is a brief attempt to sum up different approaches.

NAME	DESCRIPTION	EXAMPLE
NEW YEAR'S RESOLUTION	An attempt to change what you judge to be a negative behaviour	I'm going to go on a diet and exercise every day.

SHORT-TERM GOAL	Something to be accomplished within a specific time frame. This is primarily about us on an individual level and may well involve achievement or gain. A specific, clearly defined goal is a powerful way to get what we need.	My goal is to sort out all my tax affairs by the end of the month.
AN INTENTION	Setting a wider resolution for your health, relationship, life style, etc. Your primary aim is for you to benefit from the intention, but others may also benefit.	My intention is to find the right partner to share my life with.
LIFE INTENTION	A life intention is more likely to involve your values and the well-being of others. The statement of life intention is profoundly personal to you, and is your soul's desire for the rest of your life. In moments of confusion or doubt, it can provide focus and clarity. It serves as a guide and reminder of what is important to you on the deepest level. It can create healthy boundaries and give a profound sense of freedom and joy.	The result of a deep personal exploration.

In the second half of life there may be much that we still want to do, but in order to access our inner power we need to determine how we want to be for the rest of our lives rather than focusing exclusively on external goals. We might be aware that no matter how much we were rewarded for our achievements, there was still a hunger for more. The purpose of a growth economy (of which we are a part), is for people to want bigger, better or simply more of whatever the consumer lifestyle has to offer. But as we mature, we might start to realise that no amount of what we want, is going to satisfy our appetite in the long term. In the biographies of the rich and famous, there's often a sense of their disappointment in later life. As Isaac Newton said,

> I seem to have been only like a boy playing on the seashore, and diverting myself now and then in finding a smoother pebble or prettier shell than ordinary, while the great ocean of truth lay all undiscovered before me.

After all their achievements and glory, they had expected a greater sense of meaning to their life. They see old age and death on the horizon and realise that all the money, adoration and pleasure in the world won't amount to much as their physical and mental capabilities diminish. The 'great ocean of truth' that Newton talks about doesn't lie before us. It is inside of us and if we want to do more than find prettier shells, we would do well to make a life intention for ourselves.

Creating a Life Intention

A life intention is an immensely powerful tool that can create clarity in many difficult or complex situations. It gives us a compass point and something to hang onto when the going gets tough. It can define our boundaries so that we are able to say no if something does not align with our values. Unlike the goals we may previously have set, a life intention can create a sense of freedom that is not dependent on external circumstances. It enables us to sustain ourselves both in times of suffering and ground ourselves in the present moment. It is the link that takes us on the journey from the present moment right up to our last breath. It can also be the spark that ignites transformation.

> **Q.** Why do I need a living intention? Can't I just try to be in the moment and honour my natural instincts.
>
> **A.** We need a basic reference point so that if we get distracted, we don't veer too far off course. The Laboratory of Neuro Imaging at the University of Southern California estimates we have around 70,000 thoughts each day which is why it is good to define our deepest need. Whatever is happening, we can get back in alignment with our true values and what we want for our lives.

The invitation to you here is to connect the present moment and the final moment with an intention that can inspire you now, and all the way up to your last breath. You might want to start this process in quiet solitude or in meditation, perhaps as part of your spiritual practice or in nature. Remember that your conscious mind doesn't have all the answers. Create a space for new insights and revelations to emerge. Cultivating a statement about how you want to be now until the time of your death may take some soul searching. The living intention has to be personal and meaningful to you. It should be a creative act, and the more work that you put into forming the intention, the more powerful it will be. It is not something to grab off the shelf and for that reason there are no simple examples provided here.

> **Q.** Isn't summing up my life intentions in a couple of sentences too simplistic? Aren't I much more complex than that?
>
> **A.** We are sophisticated organisms living in a complex world. We have physical, intellectual, emotional and spiritual needs. As we grow older it is important to have clarity of purpose or we can end up like a bit of driftwood being tossed around on the ocean of circumstance. A life intention gives us the two virtues of simplicity and clarity. It's a mental decluttering that is essential in the second half of life. It gives us direction without limiting us in any way.

Creating the intention for your life may take a while, so patience is needed. It may take days, weeks or months to arrive at something that really works for you. It may be an on-going process and slowly evolve from a few random words. There is no specific format to follow but there are some key guidelines to consider.

CRITERIA FOR LIFE INTENTION	EXPLANATION
To access your inner power, the intention MUST SERVE YOU	Is it aspirational? Is it what you desire? Can you work with your shadow? (See below.)
To access your inner power, the intention MUST SERVE LIFE	The well-being of others. The community. The ecosystem.
To access your inner power, the intention MUST BE RESILIENT	Can it include this breath now, your final breath and the moments in between?
To access your inner power, the intention MUST PLEASE YOU	Does the intention sit well with you? Does it feel honest and true? Can you own it?
To access your inner power, the intention MUST BE MEMORABLE	Keep it short and pithy 15-30 words is ideal. Are the words pleasing and easy to remember. Can they be improved?
To access your inner power, the intention MUST BE BELIEVABLE	Do you believe your intention can be transformative?

We do not have to wait for some far-off time when we've got rid of all negative aspects in our character to create and realise our powerful intention. We don't have to wait until we are without blemish or fault in order to enjoy the effects of our intention.

In Buddhist philosophy the beautiful, lotus flower emerges from the muddy swamps. In other words, the mud or dirt in our lives provides the nutrients to create something beautiful. We don't have to be holy or pretentious to access our inner power. Indeed, the search for perfection can be a death sentence for the germination of the seed. To try 'photoshopping' the flaws and faults out of our character will not make us happy. We might think we are not good enough because of our grief or pain and we may try to block out the negativity in our lives. We may think our wants and desires are dysfunctional or impure and we may try to deny them, but they are part of us. We may despair at the anger, greed and stupidity in the human race, but we are not separate from it.

The Shadow and Why We Should Use It

We need all parts of our being in order to create a powerful intention that is much more than just a positive affirmation. In creating a statement, we can utilise our shadow side that sits in our unconscious mind. Carl Jung[42] maintained that everyone has a shadow which is an instinctive and irrational part that we sometimes see reflected in the behaviour of others. For example, we might think of someone as being greedy for food or money, and their grasping actions make us feel uncomfortable because we have suppressed this type of behaviour in ourselves. As we get older and take the interdependent view of life, we can explore aspects of our shadow side as they are a rich source of energy that we have suppressed. It is useful to be honest with ourselves about our shadow side and the feelings that we're not comfortable with, as it may contain the key to finding our life intention. If we are triggered by one of the qualities below, it may be a clue in the search for our life intention.

EXERCISE 7 – What Do You Hate?

Which one of the behaviours below do you most hate to see in yourself or in other people? Make a note of it in your journal and give a couple of examples if you can.

GREED: Hunger for more money, food or possessions. Never being satisfied

WEAKNESS: Fearful. Uncommitted. Foolish. Lazy. Unreliable.

ANGER: Irritable. Impatient. Suppressed rage. Want to control or dominate others.

Some degree of greed, weakness and anger seems inherent in the human condition. Modern life can easily activate these qualities which we can suppress or act on. Fortunately, we possess other qualities that provide an antidote to these more negative forces.

EXERCISE 8 – Transformational Energy

This exercise looks at how we can use any negative energy and transform it into a more positive force. How might the energy in column A be transformed by the inner power in column C? Focusing on the quality you chose in column A, write in your journal about the potential of transformation for yourself and others by using the energy in column C. How could this change affect you and your community/environment?

A	B	C
GREED	For more money, food or possessions. Never being satisfied	Gratitude Wisdom
WEAKNESS	Fearful. Uncommitted. Foolish. Lazy. Unreliable. Living in an illusion	Courage Strength
ANGER	Irritable. Impatient. Suppressed rage with the system. Want to control or dominate others.	Compassion Love Respect

Here are some examples of people who have set about identifying and transforming their shadow or negative side.

Example of transforming a sense of never having enough

Sarah felt that she didn't get enough love in her life despite the fact she admitted to having a loving partner. Both her children had moved away and had busy lives of their own, so that she only got the occasional phone call or visit. Since her own childhood Sarah has tended to see what was missing, rather than what she had. Sarah included **a profound sense of gratitude** as part of her living intention.

Example of transforming fear

Since his childhood Tony had always had a tendency towards anxiety. Now in his sixties, the underlying fear of messing things up had got worse, despite Tony having had a successful career. He felt as though there was an impending disaster around every corner. Tony worked with the words **courage and strength** in his living intention.

> ### Example of transforming anger
>
> Philip was about to step down as a trustee of a well-known charity. He was generally thought of as a kind and considerate role model to his colleagues, and yet he was aware that he had suppressed an unhealthy level of anger. This can sometimes manifest as random impatience. Philip included the words **compassion and respect** in his living intention.

> ### Example of transforming lack of confidence
>
> Sandra believes she had made some bad choices in life. Looking back, she felt whenever she got to a crossroads, she had never trusted her instincts. Her decisions in relationships and in her business were often based on the fear of doing the wrong thing. Now in pre-retirement she had put all her savings into a 'nightmare' property. Sandra included **wisdom, courage and respecting herself and others**.

Very few people are able to write down their life intention with ease. Using a few words to describe the intention for your life is an interesting challenge. You may ask yourself a hundred times; 'What is the intention for my life?' and come up with a hundred different answers. That's fine. It is a very important question and one that we need to keep asking once we're in the second half of life. If we drift into old age without being conscious of our intention, we will surely be buffeted about by other people's agenda. So just keep asking the question. What is my life intention? Ask it when you're sad and lonely! Ask it when you're happy! Ask it when you're fearful! Ask it when you feel there is no hope left. What is my life intention?

Life Intention and The Final Moment

On the deepest level we can have a life intention which will serve as a guide to the journey right up to and including the moment of our death. We don't know how long this life intention will last, of course, so it needs to be broad and powerful. It is from this intention that all other intentions, beliefs, thoughts and actions can flow. It is the source of our inner power. The place to find our life intention is the present breathe that is conscious of our final breath.

In many spiritual traditions the final moment of our life is significant. It may or may not be the gateway to another incarnation or consciousness. It is a point in time and your final moment in this world. It's safe to say there will be no more moments for you in this physical form. So, thinking back to chapter 8, how would you like to die? What emotion

THE SEED OF INTENTION

you like to be dominant as you die. How would you like it to feel?

If we use Robert Plutchik's[43] wheel of emotions we can see that there is a wide range of choice. Do we really want to leave this world with a feeling of disgust and loathing? Would anyone consciously choose to die in a state of rage, grief or terror?

Will we rage against the dying of the light? Or given the choice would we prefer to experience joy, trust or love in our last breath? According to the law of attraction if we make a strong determination to die in a state of serenity and acceptance, then that's what will happen.

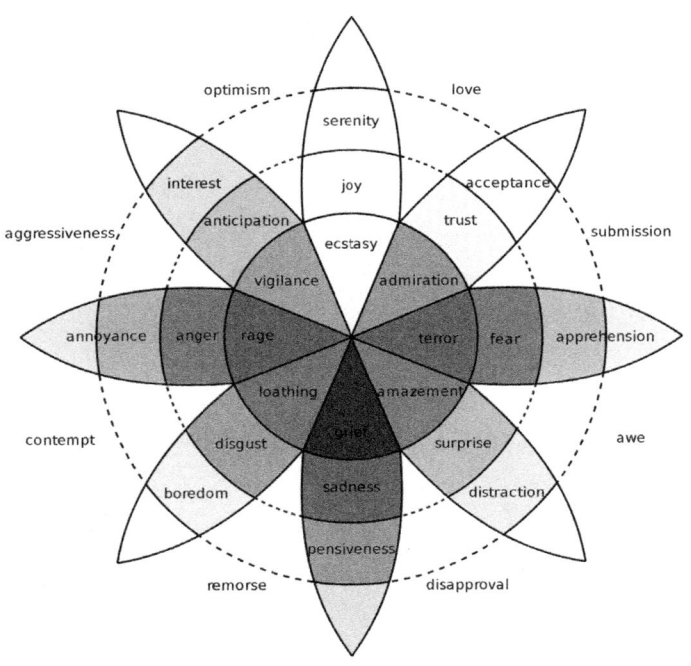

Old age and death may amplify the dominant feelings that we experience day to day. If we are annoyed and frustrated by life now, the chances are that we will even be more annoyed in our old age and in our dying.

So, knowing full well that this final moment, this last breath will definitely come to us, how do we want to feel? We can make a choice. It might sound ridiculous to say that my intention is to die experiencing joyous wisdom. Or it may sound like wishful thinking. But if we make a positive life intention, then we can start living with the possibility of joyous wisdom for all the days that we are alive and for the moment of our death. We need to be prepared. We need to be ready when the time comes. If we live for a few more months, then we can search for our inner joy and wisdom or whatever we chose. Or if we live for a few more decades with the intention of joyous wisdom each day then our death should be a wonderful occasion – something Rumi called 'our wedding with eternity.'

EXERCISE 9 – First draft of a Life Intention

So, we need to make a start with a basic statement on 15-30 words. It may help to ask yourself some of the questions listed below. You might feel your first draft is pretentious or simplistic, but this is part of the journey of inner exploration. Keep at it. Once it is written down, you can add to it or adapt it. Your inner critic may want to undermine your process. You can rip it up and start again. You can live with it and road test it, to see if it's right for you. Don't worry if it feels as if you are not getting anywhere. Keep working at it and over the weeks or months you will find the Life Intention that is true for you. Find the words that express your soul's desire for your life.

- What default emotion do you intend to feel in your old age and death?
- How do you want to serve yourself and others?
- Is there a possibility of transforming a negative element in your life to something value-creating.
- How do you want to be in the world?
- What are your core values?
- How do you want to want to be remembered?

The statement below might seem ambiguous or vague to some, but as long it has clear and profound meaning for its author, it does not matter.

My life intention is to be open and strong in order to bring healing and joy to myself and others.

Around the world great masses of people are suffering and without hope. Even if we could change the system, it would soon get replaced by another system that is prone to the same corruption and greed. Trying to change other people is a hopeless task and a waste of energy. But we really can change ourselves each day. We can re-connect with our life intention and make a difference in our environment. If we are interconnected, we can produce powerful results, no matter if we are rich or poor, healthy or sick.

Of course, we will get diverted, hijacked and spooked by any number of events. We will not always be up to scratch. We may come crashing down. We may feel shame and guilt at our failures. None of this matters, so long as we connect back to our life intention. So, once we have the seed of intention, we need to plant it with some care.

JUSTIN'S STORY: Reconnecting

After years of hard work, Justin had built up a successful design business and was starting to take life a little easier. When Justin was 53, his father died, and he was surprised by how affected he was by the death. There had been plenty of animosity between the two of them, but after the funeral, Justin started drinking like he used to thirty years ago as a student. He was shocked at the grief and the pain he felt, and in the mornings after, he was appalled by his own lack of self-control.

Justin knew he was a long way from who he wanted to be, and the living intention he had made a while back. But it was the memory of creating the intention that helped Justin come to terms with his grief in a healthier way. He sought out the support he needed, and slowly started to reconnect with the values that were important for him.

PLANTING THE SEED

Taking care to plant the intention deeply in life

Once you have written down your intention on a piece of paper, it is important to memorise it word for word. Check that you can bring the whole intention to mind at will. For some this may be easy although if this is a struggle for you, it is not a bad thing – working on it will help internalize it. Keep working on memorising your intention until you are absolutely ready to burn the piece of paper. Ideally there should be no written record of your intention, so if it is in digital form, then make sure that you delete every record of it. The intention needs to be in your mind, your heart and your soul.

Planting the seed of life intention is the opening up of a soulful connection to the universe, but it is a delicate process. Watch out for the judgmental part of you that demands perfection or the inner critic that says that whatever you do will not work out. Allow your intuitive self the freedom to work this process. You have to be brave enough to trust! There is an element of self-belief and faith in life that needs to happen with our intention.

If we have a sunflower seed, for example, but don't believe that a dried kernel weighing 0.05 grams can grow into a radiant sunflower, we probably wouldn't bother planting it. Sowing seeds requires a degree of trust in the power of nature. If we want the sunflower to grow into a healthy plant, then we should consider where best to plant it. The soil, wind and the amount of sunlight are important factors.

We could burn our written life intention unceremoniously, but to give the intention lasting and deep power we can ritualise or create a ceremony to complete this process. Ideally this will be most powerful if it takes place in nature. For some it may be a simple and sacred act in a garden, park or woodland, or by a river or on the seashore. For others it may be a more convoluted ritual that involves consulting tides, the phase of the moon and the planetary aspects. You may work alone or invite a friend or your whole community to a shamanic ritual if you like. Whatever feels right for you in order to make your prayer deep and sincere. It is a symbolic act and it is as significant as you wish to make it.

Most seeds germinate in darkness and they take time. In a world where we can access information and buy things we want in seconds, you might expect to see some results from your intention within days. It might seem as though nothing is happening but the gestation period for the intention is crucial. It needs to bed into your mind and soul. Again, this takes some self-belief and trust.

Our intention is precious. It is ours and nothing can take it away from us. It is also our choice to what extent we respect the intention. We might want to keep it to ourselves, or we might choose to tell others. Think carefully before sharing it. It is wise not to be flippant but to guard your life intention with care, and if you do share it with another, make sure that they are able to respect your commitment. Your life intention is not up for debate or superficial chat.

So now you are ready to saddle up your horse and start your journey trusting that the universe will support you. You will meet various challenges. They say you never know how strong you are until being strong is the only choice you have. There will be obstacles on the road ahead but now your inner wisdom, compassion, and courage can be activated whenever it's needed.

EXERCISE 10 – Planting the Seed

Memorise your intention. Delete all written record of the intention. Burn the paper with the intention in a way that is significant to you.

LAURIE'S STORY: Losing the power

Laurie was getting better paid work at 51 than at any other time in his life. He had had some long periods out of work in the past and regularly saw a therapist due to depression.

But more recently his face seemed to fit for casting agents in the film industry and Laurie has been on a high. One of the leads in the film told Laurie about a retreat she had just been on. She recommended the inner transformation work. As Laurie was a little in awe of the star, he booked himself a place on the next available retreat. On the next film location a few weeks later, Laurie felt like a star himself. The cast and the crew all heard about Laurie's transformation.

After that, Laurie went a year without a single casting and sunk back into a depression. He told his therapist that he felt he had been given a wonderful gift on the retreat, but had somehow given the gift away.

TENDING THE SHOOTS

Supporting your life intention, no matter what difficulties may occur

Once the seed of intention is sown it requires you to tend it with care so that it will grow strong roots and eventually produce wonderful flowers and fruits in your life. We want to see the results, but we need a degree of patience and trust. If we plant a sunflower seed in the soil, it will take a few weeks before we see the smallest shoot. Once planted, the seed doesn't need constant attention, but it does need to be nurtured on a regular basis if we're going to get the best outcome. In this chapter we are going to look at what might possibly prevent us from living our intention and what tools and practices we can develop to make sure we experience joy and fulfillment in the second half of life.

The journey through life is never straight forward, and there are many things that can occur to prevent us from living our intention. The complex and confusing world can seem like an obstacle course with many unhelpful distractions. But having planted a life intention, we get the chance to see how life works more clearly and how the negative forces can undermine us. Here are three potential pitfalls.

Fear

We can be sure of challenges and set-backs as we grow older. Ageing, loss, sickness and death are inevitable. How will we cope? Do we fear being out of control or overtaken by events? How will we respond to the problems and emotions that confront us and the emotions that might threaten to overwhelm us? Fear can trigger a closing down, resulting in a limited mindset. Fear may lead to self-doubt and down the rabbit hole of distractions and habitual behaviour that we looked at in chapter 8. On the other hand, a degree of fear may motivate us to connect with our life intention so that we can access our inner wisdom, compassion and strength. As Mahatma Gandhi said; 'Your struggles develop your strengths. When you go through hardships and decide not to surrender, that is strength.'

The Judgement of Others

In our independently-minded society, there are many unfulfilled people who want to impose a regime of separation and barriers. Ageism is just one form of discrimination that is prevalent in our youth-orientated culture. People demonise what they fear and so ageing has become one of the few remaining taboos. Ageist judgements can undermine and limit us in many ways, but with our intention deeply rooted in our life, we can develop powerful resilience to the closed minds and narrow opinions of others.

The Inner Critic

Far more dangerous than the words and actions of others is our inner critic. We may set an intention and then think; 'Who am I to do that? I'm not good enough. It won't work for me. I can never be happy.' The inner critic is armed with plenty of information and reasons why you can never be what you want to be. The inner critic's message might be that you will fail because of your childhood or the genes that you inherited. Perhaps you have tried many times before to change your life, but always reverted to self-doubt. You might suddenly doubt your life and feel it is a mistake, and so back you go to a closed mindset and fatalistic pessimism. You may be miserable, but you're comfortable with the familiarity of your misery. Your inner critic might tell you it's just trying to keep you safe. From the perspective of interdependence, there is no safety is remaining small and it is our life intention that can open up our source of power. If we are connected to our life intention, then we can change the paradigm.

Supportive Tools and Practices

While we might need patience to see the flowers and fruits of our intention, it requires more than a passive mindset. There is much that we can do to nurture the growth of our life intention. The following list of suggestions is not comprehensive but will give you a good starting point.

ACTIVITY	WHAT	WHY	HOW
CHECK-IN	Weekly, two-way process.	A quick and reliable way to connect with self and other	SEE NOTES BELOW
PRACTICE	Time and space for yourself to reflect on life.	Connects to the present moment.	Prayers, chanting mindfulness, breathing, yoga, Tai chi, etc.
NATURE	Spending time in the out-doors.	Develops sense of interconnectedness and being part of an ecosystem.	Observing seasons, plants, trees, birds, insects, etc.

COMMUNITY	Involvement in local activities.	Develop soul connection with self and others.	Volunteering Workshops Etc.
DEATH AWARENESS	Exploring the mystery of life and death without seeking answers.	Transforms fear of the unknown into energy and love for life.	Books, Death Cafes Hospice work Advanced Plan Grief Circles Older friends and relatives.
CREATIVITY	Self-exploration and expression.	Observing the inner critic. Not being afraid of the unknown. Being spontaneous.	Journaling. Painting. Singing. Drumming, etc
VERBAL CONNECTION	Listening without judgment Expressing with honesty.	Deepens humanity through openness and vulnerability.	SEE NOTES BELOW
CONSCIOUS EXERCISE	Developing a non-competitive relationship with your physicality.	Connecting with the wonder of your ageing body.	Enjoying exercise at whatever level feels right for you.

A powerful way to stay connected to your life intention is to check in on a regular basis with someone that you trust – preferably at the same time every week. The process need takes only around 20 minutes and can be done face-to-face or on-line with a friend, a relative or with anyone you feel safe to confide in.

EXERCISE 11 – A Person to Person Check In

Both parties start by agreeing that nothing that is said in the session is to be repeated outside of the session. Confidentiality is important as there needs to be a strong degree of trust. One of you asks the first question of the other, 'How are you feeling physically?' This is your chance to answer spontaneously by checking in with yourself in that moment. The more open and vulnerable you are with your reply the better. If you stumble or are lost for words, it doesn't matter. When you have explored your physical well-being or lack of it, you conclude by saying, "That's how I'm feeling physically'. This might take two or three minutes. Your confident listens without judgement and makes no comments, and then asks the next question. Once you have answered the four questions, you may thank your friend and then reverse roles and it's your turn to ask the questions. This format allows the speaker to explore how they are in the moment without analysis and it allows the listener to connect empathically.

QUESTION	TYPES OF SPONTANEOUS RESPONSES
1. How are you feeling physically?	Health. Energy levels. Sense of the physicality. Active. Tired.
2. How are you feeling mentally?	Interests. Intellectual engagement. Involvement with ideas. Learning. Reading. Lazy. Bored
3. How are you feeling emotionally?	Angry. Sad. Connected. Loving. Lonely. Anxious.
4. How are you feeling spiritually?	A chance to explore your on-going relationship with your life intention. (The other person does not need to know your life intention.)

Honest Connection

For some of us, the second half of life is an opportunity to be true to ourselves in a way that maybe wasn't possible when we were younger. Hopefully we have more freedom to communicate what we really feel. The language of independence and separation is often perfunctory. A friend asks if you're okay and it's easier and socially more acceptable to say 'I'm fine, thanks' than to express a feeling of sadness – indeed this is more or less the socially expected answer. It can be seen as anti-social or even rude to answer honestly. It's what we have always done - taken the easiest or most efficient route. It's understandable when you're struggling for survival in the busy world, but as we increasingly realise our time on this planet is finite, so we can be clearer about our true feelings. It can be surprising, uncomfortable or even shocking for those around you who are still expecting the social niceties. Expressing our true feelings makes us vulnerable to the judgments and criticism of others. It takes practice but it is empowering. We don't have to justify our feelings.

By being honest in this way, we are also enabling others to reflect on their own vulnerability and feelings. They may try to fix us or rescue us. They may try to make us feel better by projecting onto us. 'I know - that's just how I feel'. Stating how you feel in everyday situations is surprisingly empowering. And it is not just around fear and sadness. If someone is expecting us to say we're 'okay' when they ask and we tell them truthfully that we are feeling great joy, it changes from an efficient conversation to a meaningful one. If we're going to empower ourselves, we need to have meaningful connection with others and to saying 'I'm okay' doesn't convey much at all.

ADE'S STORY: Listening without Judgement

Ade looked like he had both Asian and African blood in him. He was in his early 60s but looked like he had had a hard life. In fact, Ade had spent eight years in prison for stabbing someone, but a few years ago had engaged in a transformational programme that had changed his life. Now he was working for a mentoring charity for young men who had been caught up in the criminal justice system.

Danny had been locked up twice by the time he was 20. He was wild, reckless and turbo-charged. A well-meaning teacher had tried to rescue him, but that was never going to work. Since his dad left home when he was 11 and his mum committed suicide, Danny had been on a roller coaster of drink, drugs and robbery. Social workers tried to fix him. Probation workers tried to advise him but eventually the magistrates felt it was all in vain, and that next time it would be a long sentence.

When Ade first came into contact with Danny, he wasn't triggered by any of the racist abuse he received. Ade saw a young man in pain and took nothing he said personally. Not surprisingly Danny had trust issues and he found smart ways to challenge and test Ade's patience. Over the weeks that followed Ade didn't say much but he listened. There were long silences, but Danny didn't feel he was being judged. He'd seen plenty of psychiatrists

> and therapists in the past but there was a quality to Ade's listening that helped Danny to feel safe and trusting for the first time in his life.

HARVESTING THE FLOWERS AND FRUITS

Becoming a healing elder in the face of uncertainty

In the autumn of our days there is so much richness and beauty in life. Despite the cultural horror of growing older, people are statistically much happier in the 60s and 70s than in middle age, as this graph from the Office of National Statistic shows;

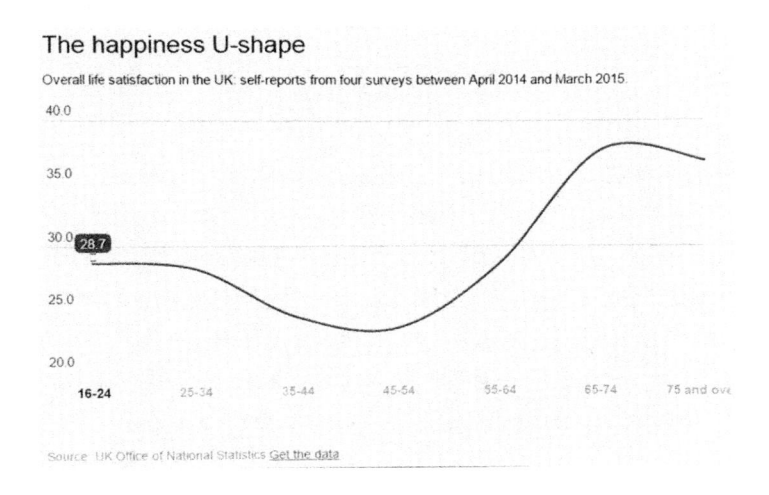

The happiness U-shape

Overall life satisfaction in the UK: self-reports from four surveys between April 2014 and March 2015.

Source: UK Office of National Statistics Get the data

If people in their early 50s realised that there was a possibility of being happier in their 90s than they are at present, perhaps there would be less anxiety in the world.

Keats was only 24 when he wrote one of the most famous poems in the English language, but it perfectly illustrates the richness of later life.

> *Season of mists and mellow fruitfulness,*
> *Close bosom-friend of the maturing sun;*
> *Conspiring with him how to load and bless*
> *With fruit the vines that round the thatch-eves run;*
> *To bend with apples the moss'd cottage-trees,*
> *And fill all fruit with ripeness to the core;*
> *To swell the gourd, and plump the hazel shells*
> *With a sweet kernel; to set budding more,*
> *And still more, later flowers for the bees,*
> *Until they think warm days will never cease,*
> *For summer has o'er-brimm'd their clammy cells.*

But how can we enjoy these fruits when we live in such a dysfunctional world? How can we relish the ripeness of our lives when there is so much suffering? How can we slow down and wonder at the mystery of life when there is so much cruelty and destruction? The field in which Keats wrote his beautiful poem is now covered by an NCP car park, so how can we savour the beauty when we are connected to such ugliness?

We may despair as we witness the greed of a few and the hunger of many, but we are not separate from it. The insatiable quest for bigger, better and more of everything is destroying our environment, but there are trace elements of greed and hunger within all of us. We live in a materialistic system that rewards insatiability, yet we are part of that system. But, we also have the capacity for appreciation. No matter what may happen, the mature adult can model gratitude every day of their life! If we live in reduced circumstances and our health is poor, we may need to search out the wonder of life. Keats knew he was dying of tuberculosis when he wrote 'To Autumn'. This was his last poem, as he had to stop writing due to financial problems, but 200 years later, we can still sense his profound sense of gratitude and wonder. Can we have just a fraction of his generosity of spirit?

The fear generated by the psychopathic tyrants who use people for their own ends, might make us feel helpless. They divide and rule and point the finger of blame at others. By excluding and manipulating, they appear strong and so the weak follow them. But from an interdependent perspective we are inextricably linked to the narcissists and the psychopaths. We are not separate from them, but we can choose the enduring power of love and compassion in the face of their tyranny. Love may seem useless when confronting such coercive power, but love and courage have shaped history as much as the brutish force that the historians and headline writers love to tell us about. In the late afternoon of life, we have the opportunity to model strong love in the face of overwhelming odds. We have to do this for ourselves, for our communities and for future generations.

The foolishness of human behaviour is staggering. The stupidity of stockpiling vast quantities of nuclear weapons, that can destroy all life on the planet at the push of a button, might make us feel hopeless, but we are connected to such foolishness. We are not separate, but we can choose to offer an eternal belief in the beauty of life and the human spirit.

There is a prejudice that holism or the theory of interdependency is the result of idealistic and woolly thinking. Some may think this 'hippy' nonsense for lazy or stupid people who are unable to compete in the cut and thrust of the capitalist marketplace. But this is reductive and out-dated thinking. It is as deluded as believing that the solar system revolves around the earth. Separation and the independent mindset have their uses, but they cannot offer us any meaningful satisfaction as we age.

Over the last 100 years or so, there has been a huge shift in the way the scientific community see the interconnectedness of all things, so there is a possibility that the way we are and the way we interact with others can also change. For thousands of years indigenous tribes around the world have valued their interconnected relationship with nature and with each other. Their relationship with plants, animals and the earth has been central to their being. As the world struggles with overwhelming problems, only a change of consciousness in each of us will save humanity, and it is those of us in the second half of life that are best placed to model this change.

No matter how 'good' we are, or how much 'work' we have done, we are not disconnected from our community, culture or country. Around the world, great masses of people are suffering. Within each community there is loss and grief. Within individuals there is the terror of old age, sickness and death. We may wish to disown the system and insulate ourselves from it, but the fact is that we are an integral part of it. There is no other world or paradise that we can flee to. No billionaires underground bunker or a colony on Mars will produce the happiness that we seek. If there was a pill that gave us immortality, we would crave the joy that we get from being mortal! Where we are right now is the best place to be, and it is from here that we can access our inner power and stop looking for solutions outside ourselves.

For many thousands of years people (especially older people) have been bemoaning the state of the world to anyone who will listen and today we have more forms of the apocalypse on offer than ever. And it is not just those of us in the second half of life that see the immense problems facing our civilisation. Many young people have lost hope in a sustainable future. As Joanna Macey says;

> "Yes, it looks bleak. But you are still alive now. You are alive with all the others, in this present moment. And because the truth is speaking in the work, it unlocks the heart. And there's such a feeling and experience of adventure. It's like a trumpet call to a great adventure. In all great adventures there comes a time when the little band of heroes feels totally outnumbered and bleak, like Frodo in Lord of the Rings or Pilgrim in Pilgrim's Progress. You learn to say 'It looks bleak. Big deal, it looks bleak.'"

The lotus plant represents the important principle of the simultaneity of cause and effect. Most plants and trees flower before they produce fruit. Think of the cherry blossom that appears in spring at least two months before the cherries appear. However, the lotus plant is different. It blooms and bears fruit at the same time which symbolises the non-duality of cause and effect. So, if we have made the cause (carefully planted a strong intention) then the effect is already lodged in our lives and it just takes the right set of circumstances for the intention to become manifest.

Once we have embraced our mortality with a life intention, we can experience unconditional happiness. No longer do we have to compromise ourselves or our values. We can liberate ourselves from the expectations of others, so that we don't have to play a role or behave in a certain way. We have the freedom to be who we want to be. There is no need to be conspicuously wise or pious. As a mature adult we have the freedom to be a benevolent fool or an irreverent joker. Once we have a powerful life intention and have accepted our own mortality, we can become vulnerable one moment and a cosmic dancer the next. We can embrace the dark and the light, the grief and the joy. We can trust our clarity of purpose and the cause we have made, so that when challenges or difficult situations arise, we can fully access our inner power.

We, who have lived through so much, know there is another way to co-exist. If a small percentage of the 15 million baby-boomers in the UK were to realise their inner power, we could transform the paradigm so that younger generations no longer saw ageing and death as a terrifying failure but as a joyful and natural part of life.

It is no good waiting for the politicians or the economists to find a solution. No new theory or scientific discovery is going to create the change that we want. It has to start with a personal revolution in each of us.

RALPH'S STORY: Shedding a skin

After being made redundant at the sixth form college, Ralph fell to pieces. He had terrible rows with his sister who told him some uncomfortable home truths. His mother died within a few months at the care home and then his partner left him. It was the perfect storm for Ralph, but as he later wrote in his journal, "seeds germinate best in the darkness".

Ralph had had two short stories published in his late 20s, and realized that in the twenty years of teaching literature at the college, he had hardly written anything. While he was documenting his personal transformation in a journal, Ralph started to explore his writing further, and discovered a sense of joy and freedom that had been missing all these years.

Today, many things have changed in Ralph's life. He feels he has – painfully at first – shed a skin. The car, the overseas holidays, the frequent meals out have all gone. Life has slowed down, but Ralph feels he has come into his own.

AFTERWORD

Many thanks for reading this book which must have been a solitary experience, but my hope is that it will lead to many more meaningful connections in your life.

In September 2020 the world seems to be at a tipping point. As inter-dependent beings can we observe the state of the world and still have a sense of hope? For millennia older people in particular have been bemoaning the state of the world, but today there are many threats to the well-being of billions of people. Never has there been more apocalyptical options available. Can we still have faith in the future of our species? Fortunately, there are examples of a fundamental change in the collective consciousness happening over a relatively short space of time.

If you had asked a hundred a fifty years ago, if women could have equal rights as men, many would not have been able to imagine such a thing as most of life was prescribed by a male agenda. It has been a long fight that is not over for many, but the struggle and the sacrifice of a few trail-blazers, like Emmiline Pankhurst meant that there has been a huge shift in consciousness around women's rights. The idea of equal rights for women has spread in some form or another to most parts of the world because of the struggle that was started by a few brave people.

A similar change in consciousness has happened with LGBT. Seventy years ago, it was seen as a disease for which you would be imprisoned. It would have been unthinkable in the 1950s that the police would turn up in pink helmets to celebrate Gay Pride.

Sixty years ago, the prevailing ethic within the medical profession was that patients should be cured and if that wasn't possible then it was seen as failure. It was acceptable to lie to patients about their prognosis which was a terrible way to treat people at the end of their lives. One nurse by the name of Cecily Saunders[44] thought people at the end of their lives should be given effective pain management and insisted that dying people needed dignity, compassion, and respect. In 1967 she founded the first hospice that started a movement that has spread all over the world. She and a few other pioneers such as Elizabeth Kubler-Ross have had a huge impact on how we think about death and dying. It is a change in consciousness that very few could have predicted.

More recently Zalman Schachter-Shalomi, a Jew and an unconventional Rabbi pioneered the practice of working with fellow seniors on coming to spiritual terms with ageing and becoming mentors for younger adults. It's a movement that is slowing spreading in parts of America and will hopefully take root in Europe. Of course, there are many mentoring organisations but how many of them start by coming to terms with ageing and death?

Today is my 71st birthday and I'm passionate about seeing a shift in the ageing paradigm before I die. I believe a fundamental shift in consciousness around ageing is possible and is a key ingredient for a healthy society. If older people can come to terms with ageing and their mortality, then the effect on the well-being of younger generations would be substantial. There would be less fear and more appreciation of life and nature.

It is imperative that people in the second half of life with different skill sets and experiences start to come together to look at and challenge our terror of ageing and death. What can we bring and what legacy could we offer?

If you are interested in exploring the power of ageing further and connecting up with others, there is some recommending reading and some website that may be useful. And please, if this book has been useful or you have any thoughts you would like to share, please go to our website, powerofageing.org. You will find courses and resources to support you in your liberation from the tyranny of separation and fear.

APPENDIX

PLANNING FOR THE END OF LIFE

What is important is that you have written down your plan and that those important to you and health and social care professionals involved in your care know where your plan is kept. Of course, you can (and should) review your plan to make sure it reflects your current situation and wishes.

Advance Statement

An Advance Statement allows you to make general statements, describing your wishes and preferences about future care should you be unable to make or communicate a decision or express your preferences at the time. You may want it to reflect religious or other beliefs and important aspects of your life. You can include things such as food and drink preferences; type of clothes you like to wear; music, TV or DVD preferences, or whether you like a bath or a shower etc. You can say who you would like to visit you or be consulted about your care.

It is not legally binding but should be taken into account when those who are taking care of you are considering your best interests. There are no formal guidelines for making an Advance Statement but it's a good idea to write your name, date of birth and address on the document and to also sign and date it. Including your personal information and signature helps to confirm that it's your wishes that are written down.

You can also use it to specify any people you'd like to be consulted – Proxy Spokes Person/People – when decisions are being made on your behalf. However, doing this doesn't mean that a healthcare professional has to follow what that person says. The only way to give another person the legal power to make health or care decisions on your behalf is by making a Lasting Power of Attorney

Advance Decision to Refuse Treatment

An advance decision to refuse treatment also known as an advance decision, an ADRT, or a living will is a decision you can make now to refuse a specific type of treatment at some time in the future should you lose mental capacity e.g. severe dementia, a stroke etc. Examples of treatments which can be refused include, but are not limited to Cardiopulmonary Resuscitation, Mechanical or Artificial Ventilation, Artificial Nutrition and Hydration and Antibiotics. It is legally binding and to be valid must be made when the person has mental capacity and be signed, dated and witnessed. It must include the words I maintain this refusal even if my life is at risk or shortened as a result.

Do Not Attempt Cardiopulmonary Resuscitation (DNACPR)

A Do Not Attempt Cardio Pulmonary Resuscitation form is a document issued and signed by a doctor, which tells your medical team not to attempt cardiopulmonary resuscitation (CPR). It's not a legally binding document. Instead, it helps you to communicate to the healthcare professionals involved in your care that CPR shouldn't be attempted. If you decide to have one, it's a good idea to also to make this a refusal in your advance decision. This will mean that your wishes are more likely to be followed if you lack capacity to make decisions.
https://www.resus.org.uk/
Hermione Elliott, Director of *Living Well Dying Well*, talking about CPR
https://www.youtube.com/watch?v=GQ6AB0uLR58&t=26s

Treatment Escalation Plan (TEP)

TEPs are in operation in some NHS Trusts. It includes both treatments you may and may not want. A TEP form is a way of your doctor recording your individual treatment plan, focusing on which treatments she/he believes may or may not be most helpful for you. A variety of treatments can be considered, such as antibiotics, artificial feeding or ventilation of your lungs. It is not legally binding. It is important that you ensure that your Doctor has consulted with you regarding the completion of the form so that you understand it and it reflects what you want.

Lasting Power of Attorney (LPA)

A Lasting Power of Attorney (LPA) allows you to give someone you trust the legal power to make decisions on your behalf in case you later become unable to make decisions for yourself. The person who makes the LPA is known as the 'donor' and the person given the power to make decisions is known as the 'attorney'.

There are two different types of LPA: 1. An LPA for Property and Financial Affairs covers decisions about money and property. 2. An LPA for Health and Welfare covers decisions about health and personal welfare.

You can choose to have just an Advance Decision to Refuse Treatment, just an LPA for Health & Welfare, or both. An LPA for Health & Welfare is broader in remit than an Advance Decision (it can include care arrangements, dietary preferences, etc). It can cover the same ground insofar as it addresses your refusals of treatment. If you choose to have both an Advance Decisions and an LPA for Health & Welfare it is important to ensure that they work together and that one does not invalidate the other.

LPAs can be undertaken by a Solicitor or can be done by you on-line at the Gov UK website https://www.gov.uk/power-of-attorney/overview.

Proxy Spokes Person/People

For when decisions are being made on your behalf should you lack capacity. These would be a person/people with whom you have communicated your wishes choices and preferences. However, doing this doesn't mean that a healthcare professional has to follow what that person says. The only way to give another person the legal power to make health or care decisions on your behalf is by making a Lasting Power of Attorney.

Funerals

There is useful information on all the options and choices available at:
https://www.goodfuneralguide.co.uk/

Wills

There is no requirement for a will to be drawn up or witnessed by a solicitor so an individual can make a will themselves. It is certainly advisable though to use a solicitor to make sure it will have the effect you want.

Digital Legacy

This is the consideration of what you want to happen with your all your accounts, blogs, social networking identities and digital files that will be left online when you die. More Information can be found here:
https://digitallegacyassociation.org/wp-content/uploads/2015/10/Digital-Legacy-Association-Resource-Links.pdf

Organ and Tissue Donation

https://www.organdonation.nhs.uk/
Whole Body Donation
https://www.hta.gov.uk/donating-your-body

Notes based on material kindly provided by Sarah Goodman, an End of life doula.
https://www.sarah-goodman.com/

FURTHER READING

Applewhite, Ashton. *This Chair Rocks: A Manifesto Against Ageism* Celadon Books, 2020

Becker, Ernest. *The Denial of Death*. New York: Free Press 1973

Hillman, James. *A Blue Fire: Selected writings by James Hillman*. Harper Perennial 1989

Hollis, James. *The Middle Passage: From Misery to Meaning in Mid Life*. Toronto: Inner City Books, 1993

Ikeda, Daisaku; Saito, Katsuji; Endo, Takanori; Suda, Haruo *The Wisdom of the Lotus Sutra. Vol. 1.* World Tribune Press 2000

James, John. W; Friedman, Russell. *The Grief Recovery Handbook*. William Morrow Paperbacks 2017

Jenkinson, Stephen. *Die Wise: A Manifesto for Sanity and Soul*. North Atlantic Books, 2015

Jung, C.G. *Memories, Dreams, Reflections*. New York: Vintage Books, 1965

Kübler-Ross, Elisabeth. *On Death and Dying*. Scribner, 2014

Levine, Stephen. *Healing into Life and Death*. Anchor, 1989

Macy, Joanna; Brown, Molly Young. *Coming Back to Life*. New Society Publishers, 2014

Mannix, Dr. Kathryn. *With the End in Mind*. William Collins 2019

Midgley, Mary *The Myths We Live By.* Routledge 2011

Moody, Harry R.; Carroll, David. *The Five Stages of the Soul*. Anchor, 1998

Pevny, Ron. *Conscious Living Conscious Aging.* Atria Books, 2014

Plotkin, Bill. *Nature and the Human Soul*. New World Library., 2008

Ram Dass, Ram; Bush, Miraba. *Walking Each Other Home: Conversations on Loving and Dying.* Sounds True, 2018

Robinson, John C. *The Three Secrets of Aging: A Radical Guide.* O-Books, 2012

Schachter-Sahlomi, Zalman; Miller Ronald S. *From Age-ing to Sage-ing: A Revolutionary Approach to Growing Older.* Grand Central Publishing, 2014

RECOMMENDED WEBSITES

https://www.life-stage.org/
Course, workshops and support materials

https://charleseisenstein.org/
Writer, philosopher, Mathematician. Plenty of free materials around the culture of separation.

https://www.preposterousuniverse.com/
Web site of Sean Carroll. theoretical physicist, specializing in quantum mechanics, gravitation, cosmology.

https://www.sgi.org/
Soka Gakkai International – Buddhism in Action for Peace

https://www.ageing-better.org.uk/
Working to help people enjoy later life

https://eol-doula.uk/contact-us/
Talk to an End of Life Doula who will support you to prepare your plan.

Endnotes

1. Only in retrospect can we say when the second half of life is. The life span of men and women in the UK combined is 81.05 years which means that according to statistics the second life starts when you're a few months over 40. *Office of National Statistics*

PREFACE

2. An End of Life Doula is there to support a person, and those that they love, with a terminal diagnosis. We work in the person's home as well as Hospices, Hospitals and Care Homes. We are there for the frail, elderly and those living with dementia too. https://eol-doula.uk/

CHAPTER 1

3. We breathe about 960 breaths an hour, 23040 breaths a day. www.heraldtribune.com – every breath you take

4. In 1820 the life expectancy in the UK was 40. In 1925 the life expectancy in the UK was 58. In 2020 the life expectancy in the UK was 81. https://www.statista.com/statistics

CHAPTER 2

5. Below are the ages you peak at everything throughout life according to Chris Weller and Skye Gould who compiled the list from a range of scientific studies.

    optimum time for …
    learning a new language is 7
    brain processing power is 18
    remembering names is 22
    muscle strength is 25

running a marathon is 28
peak a bone mass is 30
remembering faces is 30
making a Nobel-Prize winning discovery is 48
arithmetic skills is 50
https://www.businessinsider.com/best-age-for-everything

6 **Reductionsim** The Holism-Reductionism Debate: In Physics, Genetics, Biology, Neuroscience, Ecology, and Sociology by Gerard M Verschuuren CreateSpace Independent Publishing Platform 2017)

7 **Quarks** A quark is a type of elementary particle and a fundamental constituent of matter. Quarks combine to form composite particles called hadrons, the most stable of which are protons and neutrons, the components of atomic nuclei. All commonly observable matter is composed of up quarks, down quarks and electrons.
en.wikipedia.org › wiki › Quark
https://www.livescience.com/45344-facts-about-quarks.html

8 Quantum mechanics, science dealing with the behaviour of matter and light on the atomic and subatomic scale. It attempts to describe and account for the properties of molecules and atoms and their constituents—electrons, protons, neutrons, and other more esoteric particles such as quarks and gluons. These properties include the interactions of the particles with one another and with electromagnetic radiation (i.e., light, X-rays, and gamma rays).
Gordon Leslie Squires – Lecturer in Physics, University of Cambridge

9 Edward Norton Lorenz (1917 –2008) was an American mathematician and meteorologist who established the theoretical basis of weather and climate predictability. His discovery of deterministic chaos "profoundly influenced a wide range of basic sciences and brought about one of the most dramatic changes in mankind's view of nature since Sir Isaac Newton," according to the committee that awarded him the 1991 Kyoto Prize for basic sciences in the field of earth and planetary sciences

10 R Peters – Postgraduate medical journal, 2006 – pmj.bmj.com

11 salary peaks at 39 for women and 48 for men
    https://www.businessinsider.com/best-age-for-everything

12 Abraham Harold Maslow (1908 –1970) was an American psychologist who was best known for creating Maslow's hierarchy of needs, a theory of psychological health predicated on fulfilling innate human needs in priority, culminating in self-actualization.

13 Total number of suicides in the UK & Republic of Ireland, there were 6,859 suicides in 2018.
    Suicide facts and figures | Samaritans
    www.samaritans.org › about-samaritans › research-policy

14 In 1976, the ecologist Arthur Cain, one of Dawkins's tutors at Oxford in the 1960s, called it a "young man's book" (which Dawkins points out was a deliberate quote of a commentator on the New College, Oxford philosopher A.J. Ayer's *Language, Truth, and Logic* (1936)). Dawkins noted that he had been "flattered by the comparison, [but] knew that Ayer had recanted much of his first book and [he] could hardly miss Cain's pointed implication that [he] should, in the fullness of time, do the same.' https://en.wikipedia.org/wiki/The_Selfish_Gene.

CHAPTER 3

15 **Mirror Neurons** Giacomo Rizzolatti and Vittorio Gallese discovery is brilliantly explained by Jeremy Rifkin who investigates the evolution of empathy and the profound ways that it has shaped our development and our society.
    YouTube RSA ANIMATE: The Empathic Civilisation

CHAPTER 4

16 The cosmetic surgery industry in the UK is currently worth around £3.6 billion, and beauty treatments such as Botox and dermal fillers account for 9 out of 10 procedures, with a worth of around £2.75 billion. These figures are impressive and show just how popular non-surgical treatments are, but the one worry is the fact that the industry is almost entirely

unregulated. This means that treatments can be provided by anyone, regardless of their knowledge, expertise or qualification. https://www.harleystreetaesthetics.com/blog/dr-kremers-blog

The number of women in the United States aged between 19 and 34 receiving Botox treatments has risen by 41% since 2011. Men seeking out the treatment is also on the rise, with them accounting for 10% of all users and leading Botox for men to now being called "Brotox".

The American Society for Aesthetic Plastic Surgery (ASAPS)

17   Mary Midgley, who died aged 99, was an important writer on ethics, the relations of humans and animals, our tendency to misconstrue science, and the role of myth and poetry. From the mid-1970s onwards she published many books and articles in which she identified the limitations of only trying to understand things by breaking them down into smaller parts and losing sight of the many ways in which parts are dependent on the wholes in which they exist. These atomist and reductive approaches are particularly unhelpful when it comes to human self-understanding and, in trenchant and witty style, Midgley pointed the way to a saner and more helpful overview of ourselves and our world. From Jane Heal's obituary of Mary Midgley in *The Guardian* 12.10. 2018

18   British Social Attitudes survey for 2018 found that 52% of the public say they do not belong to any religion, compared with 31% in 1983. The number of people identifying as Christian has fallen from 66% to 38% over the same period. https://www.bsa.natcen.ac.uk/

CHAPTER 5

19   *The Rites of Passage* Arnold van Gennep University of Chicago Press; Second Edition 2019

20   Professor Manu Ampim https://manuampim.com/

21   Land diving is a ritual performed by the young men of the southern part of Pentecost Island, Vanuatu. The precursor

to bungee jumping, men jump off wooden towers around 20 to 30 meters high, with two tree vines wrapped around the ankles.

22 *Russian Fairy Tales* (Illustrated) by Alexander Afanasyev (Author), The Planet; Illustrated Edition

23 *Parzival* (Penguin Classics) Paperback – 28 Aug. 1980 by Wolfram von Eschenbach

24 Joseph Campbell's classic cross-cultural study of the hero's journey has inspired millions and opened up new areas of research and exploration. Originally published in 1949, the book hit the New York Times best-seller list in 1988 when it became the subject of The Power of Myth, a PBS television special. *The Hero with a Thousand Faces.* Joseph Campbell Princeton Bollingen; 1972

CHAPTER 6

25 *On Grief and Grieving: Finding the Meaning of Grief Through the Five Stages of Loss.* 2014 by Elisabeth Kubler-Ross David Kessler Simon & Schuster UK; Reissue Edition 2014

26 In a study of 401 people published in the Journal of Psychosomatic Research, grateful people tended to fall asleep more quickly and sleep longer, undisturbed by negative thoughts. The study, by Alex Mathew Wood of the London School of Economics, was the first to show a direct correlation between gratitude and better sleep.

27 Joanna Macy PhD, is a scholar of Buddhism, general systems theory, and deep ecology. A respected voice in the movements for peace, justice, and ecology, she interweaves her scholarship with five decades of activism. The author of more than twelve books, she is the root teacher of the Work That Reconnects.

CHAPTER 7

28 *The Human Brain in Numbers: A Linearly Scaled-up Primate Brain*, Suzana Herculano-Houzel 2009
Published on-line by Frontiers in Human Neuroscience
https://www.frontiersin.org/

29 *Information-Consciousness-Reality: How a New Understanding of the Universe Can Help Answer Age-Old Questions of Existence* James B. Glattfelder. Springer 2019

30 Sean Carroll is a theoretical physicist specializing in quantum mechanics, gravity, and cosmology. He is a research professor in the Walter Burke Institute for Theoretical Physics in the California Institute of Technology Department of Physics.
His website https://www.preposterousuniverse.com is a great source of information

31 The Lakota people or the people of Standing Rock are one of the first original Native American tribes who inhabited the North Americas before the arrival of Europeans.
https://www.lakotamall.com

32 Rumi (Author), Coleman Barks (Translator) Penguin Classics 2004

33 *The Essential Rilke* by Rainer Maria Rilke (Author), Galway Kinnell (Translator), Ecco Press; Rev ed. Edition (3 Feb. 2007)

CHAPTER 8

34 Hagakure (Bushido), *The Way of the Samurai*, Yamamoto Tsunetomo, translated by William Scott Wilson.) Classics Press (16 April 2019)

35 The term originally comes from the opening lines of the Book of Ecclesiastes in the Bible: 'Vanity of vanities, saith the Preacher, vanity of vanities, all is vanity.' Vanitas are closely related to memento mori still lifes which are artworks that remind the viewer of the shortness and fragility of life (memento mori is a Latin phrase meaning 'remember you must die') and include symbols such as skulls and extinguished candles. However vanitas still-lifes also include other symbols such as musical instruments, wine and books to remind us explicitly of the vanity (in the sense of worthlessness) of worldly pleasures and goods.
https://www.tate.org.uk

36 Approximately 418,000 people live in care homes (Laing and Buisson survey 2016). This is 4% of the total population aged 65 years and over, rising to 15% of those aged 85 or more.

37 Short film about Death Café's Interviews with Adam Duncan, Spencer Thomas and Sarah Goodman www.powerofageing.com

38 *Being Mortal: Illness, Medicine and What Matters in the End* Profile Books 2015

39 Dudjom Lingpa (1835–1904) was a Tibetan meditation master and spiritual teacher He stands out from the norm of Tibetan Buddhist teachers in the sense that he had no formal education, nor did he take ordination as a monk or belong to any established Buddhist school or tradition of his time.

40 Sam Keen a professor of philosophy wrote the words in his introduction to *The Denial of Death* by Ernest Becker, which won the Pulitzer Prize in 1974. The book is brilliant and impassioned answer to the 'why' of human existence. In bold contrast to the predominant Freudian school of thought, Becker tackles the problem of the vital lie – man's refusal to acknowledge his own mortality.
Souvenir Press; Main Edition 2020

CHAPTER 9

41 In 1891 Californian author and humorist Prentice Mulford used the term Law of Attraction in his essays *Some Laws of Health and Beauty and Good And Ill Effects of Thought*. In 1897 Ralph Waldo Trine wrote *In Tune with the Infinite*. In the second paragraph of chapter 9 he writes, "The Law of Attraction works unceasingly throughout the universe, and the one great and never changing fact in connection with it is, as we have found, that like attracts like."

42 Carl Jung 1875–1961
The Jungian shadow can include everything outside the light of consciousness and may be positive or negative. Because one tends to reject or remain ignorant of the least

desirable aspects of one's personality, the shadow is largely negative. There are, however, positive aspects that may also remain hidden in one's shadow (especially in people with low self-esteem, and anxieties. "Everyone carries a shadow," Jung wrote, "and the less it is embodied in the individual's conscious life, the blacker and denser it is."

43 Robert Plutchik (1927 –2006) was professor emeritus at the Albert Einstein College of Medicine and adjunct professor at the University of South Florida. He received his Ph. D. from Columbia University and he was also a psychologist.

AFTERWORD

44 Dame Cicely Mary Strode Saunders OM DBE FRCS FRCP FRCN (1918 –2005) was an English nurse, social worker, physician and writer. She is noted for her work in terminal care research and her role in the birth of the hospice movement, emphasising the importance of palliative care in modern medicine.

The undead

Trust woods the heads!

closed mindset
ingrained habits
             opinions.

Vast untapped resources

To be the most I can be

celebration over
initiation
                    time to
                         deeper
we need space
breathe into   profound
appreciation.   fortitude

Random impatience?